Community Management Frameworks (SPAN and CARGO) created during employment are used by permission of Higher Logic.

First edition

ISBN: 978-1-7782942-1-1

Website: https://adrianspeyer.com
Cover Design: Wayne Kehoe
Editing and Typesetting: Yellow Barn Literary

The Accidental Community Manager

A Guide to Building a Successful B2B Community

Adrian Speyer

Dedication

I dedicate the book to my wife, Orit. Her cheerleading and tireless support are the main reasons this book made it into the world.

I'd also like to dedicate this to my family, friends, and colleagues, who pushed me forward. Their energy and encouragement kept me going and helped to make this book a reality.

It's finally here, world! Enjoy!

Contents

Introduction

I was once like you. I fell into the community role — and became an accidental community manager. However, I was lucky to have a core skill. From being a short-order cook to my time in sales, marketing, and beyond, it was always about building relationships. At its core, this is the essence of community-building. Whatever you did before, you likely have a ton of skills that will be useful in this new role — you just need some help adapting them.

This is why I wrote this book. It's for the person who falls into the role and needs to figure things out. In this book, there are a bunch of personal stories, but I'll also be sharing a ton of practical information to get you going in the right direction.

Where did I learn all this stuff? I have been building communities for more than fifteen years, and for the last nine years, I've been working at Higher Logic Vanilla, a Software as a Service (SaaS) community platform. My main objective from day one has been creating connections with our customers, potential customers, allies, partners, and strangers. This book is tied to my own experience, mainly in the business-to-business (B2B) market. It's also informed by my time working with hundreds of brands and companies in creating, launching, and supercharging their communities.

For this reason, I should note that the main focus of this book will be community, translated into a branded online forum. I believe you write about what you know, and I know forums. Regardless of where you build community, I think you'll find elements, concepts, and ideas helpful to any of your community-building endeavours.

Finally, I wanted to show you that you are not alone. In these pages, I share a ton of mistakes, failures, and lessons learned. I've done this so you don't have to face the same fate without warning. Sit back, relax, and read all about them in your comfy chair, at the beach, or in your bed. Skip to the spots that you need or read it cover to cover. This book comes from my own 10,000 hours of learning and building hundreds of communities from scratch, migrations, relaunches, and everything in between. In short, this book is a collection of my wisdom for one low price. What a deal!

And so, welcome, my fellow accidental community managers! Let's have some fun, learn, inspire, and build great communities. Oh, and don't worry, I'll be with you every step of the way. Onward to your success!

— Adrian Speyer Montreal, Quebec, June 2022

Chapter 1: Welcome to the Club!

Let me tell you a secret. Imposter syndrome — feeling like you're a fraud about to be discovered — is normal. Even community experts feel this way sometimes — I know because we talk about this amongst ourselves. Please don't let this cripple you. You probably already have a ton of beneficial skills that will make you a great community builder.

If you're coming from a support or marketing role, not only do you understand the important business jargon or the key things that matter to stakeholders, but you've likely also been selected for your people skills and ability to connect with others. Even if you're not an expert, you will undoubtedly get the chance to build upon the natural skills you already possess.

Certainly, I will be focused on the B2B use case in these pages, but even with a humanities degree, right out of school, you have useful skills — from knowing how to do research, working on group projects, or making connections between different disciplines. Heck, I have a degree in American History, but I doubled down on learning all I could about marketing in my early career. Curiosity and willingness to learn are all you need.

Also, you don't need to be an outgoing extrovert to be a great community manager. As a matter of fact, many of the best, and most effective, community professionals I know are the biggest *in-person* introverts you'd ever meet. *Online*, they are huge extroverts, willing to share and welcome you with open arms to this club. The world of professional community builders is very collaborative. Yes, there may be lots of us, but many of us work in small teams or even as a team of one. For this reason, we try to be extra supportive of one another. No other role I've ever had has been as welcoming. If you get stuck, ask for help in any community for community managers or post on social media under the #cmgr or #community hashtag, and you will see how the cavalry arrives.

Now, before we begin, I am now going to ask you to do an exercise with me. I know, I know, you didn't think you would have homework so soon. However, trust me, this is an exercise to show you that you're not an imposter. You have a ton of skills. So come along and follow.

Think about your past work experiences and all the things you've done. Take a piece of paper and write down the following: all the excellent skills you have and the technology you've used. List the things you thought you did well or were responsible for. Go ahead. I'll still be here. Yes, I mean you. Trust me, please, and write this down. Oh fine, if you don't want to write it down, just think about it — deeply. Oh, and don't let humility or modesty stand in your way. Please.

Let's consider this list you've made. You will now lead a group of like-minded individuals gathering and facilitating their journey. You will be the company's face, internally and externally. How can you use these skills to be that community person? Let's look at some examples you may have written down:

- Reporting or Storytelling: Super essential for keeping stakeholders in the loop.
- Writing: Creating great content is important to not only communicate but engage others.
- Social Media: You've may have already created your personal brand and shared your passion, now you have a chance to bring what you learned to the table for your professional career.

- Math: Being able to do statistics or analyze numbers can help you gather deep insights.
- Support: You've practiced the art of talking to people who may not always be happy or are simply frustrated, and you've walked that fine line, oh, so many times.

Your list may be different or not have any of the items I listed above. The main idea is that you have skills that apply to this community role. You are not as inexperienced as you think. It will just be about applying your skills in new ways.

Sometimes I hear people comment that community can be a stepping-stone to another role in an organization. I feel the opposite. By the end of this book (I hope), you'll see that a community role is actually a career path of its own. You are at the heart of the customer experience. You are doing real advocate marketing. You are doing the crucial frontline PR work. You are an essential piece in reducing frustration as customers seek self-support. Even if those in your company can't recognize it yet, when you're done with this book, I hope you will have the confidence to show them how community is the heart of their engine. You are the master connector, bringing your customer's voice to all places that matter within your organization.

Unlike many other roles, being a community manager is a role many people can do, though some do it better than others. Very few people go to school for this or dream of being a community manager as a little kid. This is not a role that needs some specialized unattainable talent. If you want to help others succeed, if you can listen well, if you can show empathy, and you come into a position with a positive attitude to help others, nothing can stop you. It's not about technology; it's about maturity, temperament, and emotions.

How do you feel about what I laid out for the future? Are you scared because you lack some skills? Please don't panic. No community manager was able to do this error-free and without issue from the start. We share these stories of failure during late-night drinks. So, even if this is your first community job out of school — be nice to yourself. This takes time. However, you'll see quickly, this is the best career ever. This is a job where you're always learning. Best of all, when you get your community humming, it will be a rewarding career, helping others unlock their potential and do better things because of the spaces you build. How does that sound?

Phew! I'm glad we had this little talk, and I will leave you with a small thought. Whenever you have a fear of "I can't do this," remember this: You can, and will, be successful. Why? Because you cared. You cared enough to get and read this book, and to me, if you care enough to make yourself better, and you want to be successful, then you are most of the way there.

Okay, what do you think? Are you ready? I know I'm fired up! Let's make this happen. You've got thousands of other community professionals cheering you on, and I'm happy to officially invite you to the club!

Chapter 2: My Own Journey

The first online community I ever joined led to me getting banned within 10 seconds. The year was 1989. My internet access consisted of a dial-up modem and the CompuServe interface. At the time, I had a mighty 486 IBM with 64 MB RAM. It was a massive upgrade from our Commodore 64, which was showing its age. And while Q*bert was fun to play, it was time for more exciting games.

So, there I was, exploring the new interwebs and this thing called a BBS (bulletin board system). Through this text-based software, you could talk to anyone in the world about any specific topic in real time. The sysop (system operator) oversaw the board. In forum speak, we would now call them a "forum administrator." The sysop was in charge of the server (where the BBS was hosted), and of course, they would create rules members were to follow.

Eventually, I found what I thought was a cool space and joined. My first post to the group was:

"Hi all! I'm from Montreal. Anyone else enjoying the crappy weather?"

I was banned. Instantly.

At first, I didn't realize what had happened. I could still see replies to my comment, but I could not respond. I created another account and contacted the sysop for help. They told me I had broken the rules by using "foul language" and that I had been banned. I pleaded my case and apologized for my mistake. However, instead of a human, I got an automated message informing me I was banned again for creating this new account to plead my case.

As a 13-year-old boy, the essential prototype for a troll shithead, I created a third account. I sent a message to the sysop with the kind of words I felt were *worthy* of being banned as foul language. Well, at least the best a 13-year-old could think of, and somehow it made sense in my head to get my money's worth for being banned. Predictably, I was booted from the server.

This experience made me want to be in charge, rather than being a passive participant. I also felt I could be better as an owner. This led me to create my own BBS, with only one rule. "Treat everyone better than you wish to be treated." It was the platinum rule taught to me in elementary school, and I tried my best to follow it. Well, except for the time I just shared, when, I must admit, I was a total dick. However, having my own BBS, I received a good lesson — a fair amount of people don't abide by the platinum rule either. I got my own fill of trolls, shitheads, and keyboard tough guys. It led me to understand that being a sysop wasn't all glitz and glamour. However, it wasn't all bad, either, and I made friends from all over the world. You have to remember, this was a time before many of us saw the dark side of the internet — so my formative years were forged in the innocence of the good things the internet could facilitate.

Fast-forward a couple of years. By the last year of high school, computers had become more powerful, and connecting with others became easier. I moved on to building communal spaces with forum software, instead of the plain BBS. From the 1990s to the mid-2000s, there wasn't a forum software I had not tried.

In 2007, I discovered a company called Lussumo. They had this forum product called Vanilla Forums. It didn't have the features of the other forum packages, but it had the basics, and was just dead simple to install and use. The other forums had so many files, dials, and knobs. All I wanted was something easy to run, where my friends and I could connect. Vanilla fit the bill by getting out of the way and letting me create the space I wanted and, most importantly, my way.

Mark O'Sullivan and Todd Burry, the cofounders of Vanilla, were very accessible. They were generous in sharing their ideas and thoughts on how to build great communities. It wasn't hard to be excited by what Vanilla was building. Not only had they built a strong community, but they were super transparent. Mark would share their journey in building Vanilla, and the decisions they were making, on his blog, and it was fascinating. Eventually, the company they had named Lussumo changed its name to Vanilla. The community came along for the ride as they headed to Techstars in Colorado in 2009 and eventually launched what would become known as Vanilla 2.

In my spare time, I would tinker with Vanilla Forums. Not only did I learn basic programming because of Vanilla, but I also saw how they created an open source community. I started taking my community-building a bit more seriously as well. My most popular communities then were for people who shared a passion for fast food and another one I created for hockey. I never made enough to quit my day job, but I made enough money from Google AdSense to cover my hosting costs.

These projects also gave me an outlet for a passion I hadn't gotten the chance to explore. After university, I wanted to learn more about computers, but I had a more pressing concern about paying the rent. So tinkering with Vanilla Forums and other open-source projects became a hobby while I was building my career.

I don't want to bore you with my work history, but I think it was foundational in giving me lots of lessons that I would later use to become a better community builder. It began in 1999, when I got a tremendous entry-level opportunity in marketing at a multi-billion-dollar company. As someone fresh out of school with a university degree in history, it was the best business education I could ever ask for. I took every opportunity to learn and quickly moved up in the company. Eventually, I became a product manager and was finally promoted into a business development manager role. I got tons of world-class training on learning styles, negotiating, and managing people. It would also prepare me for my future work. I learned about reporting, talking to stakeholders, calculating margin, and the importance of measuring return on investment (ROI) and tracking key performance indicators (knowledfs).

In the early 2000s, I was also web obsessed. In my spare time, I spent countless hours building websites, running communities, and learning all I could about search engine optimization (SEO). I tested things again and again. I read all I could find about analytics and website building. I taught myself HTML, CSS, JavaScript and PHP. Finding a deep passion for analytics, I connected with Matthieu Aubry, founder of Piwik (now Matomo), an open-source analytics package. In my spare time, I worked with him to build their community, administer their forums, and do marketing work. Soon, the worlds of my marketing and digital work would collide.

In the summer of 2009, while on a company business trip, I had gotten wind that the corporate website would undergo significant changes. In the past, I had volunteered for special web projects, but this was a new and huge revamp of the online business. They were looking for talent from within the company, who could bring their business skills to supercharge a new online project. I jumped at the chance. Finally, all those years of self-learning and hands-on testing would give me a chance to shine.

A year into being a marketing manager for our corporate website, I was called into a meeting. The decision had been made that one of our business units needed a forum for a new launch, and there was not a lot of time. My manager and I were tasked to find the most appropriate solution as quickly as possible.

However, beyond being directed to find a solution, I did not have a clear understanding of the purpose of the community. When I asked, I was told they just needed a spot for members to connect and share documents.

I wrote down all I could from the meeting. I already knew who I loved for this project. I placed Vanilla Forums at the top of my list. Then I found the most expensive enterprise solution I could find — on purpose. I then outlined how Vanilla could give us all we needed at a fraction of the cost. I sent the email off.

Long story short, Vanilla was not selected — and in hindsight, I understand why. It was 2010, and Vanilla was a small company. My boss was considering risks I wasn't, such as that we were a multi-billion-dollar company, and Vanilla was a brand-new start-up.

In the end, Jive and Awareness Networks were selected. At this time, they had a better story, so I can't blame my company for being so cautious, although I am sure the Vanilla of today would easily win the bid. How times have changed.

With a new deadline approaching, we moved fast. We were impressed by the Jive demo, but they shot themselves in the foot when they misquoted us, by forgetting a zero on their proposal. Instead of the platform costing us five figures, it would be over $100,000. What had made it worse is that they waited too long for the correction, and it was hard to go back to our management with this new figure.

So, due to lack of time and serendipity, Awareness was the winner. They were cheap by comparison, at $36,000 a year. They also had an impressive list of customers, like McDonald's and Coca-Cola, so we felt comfortable with them. However, as I played with their forum platform in the sandbox created for us, I began to notice many of Vanilla's standard features were missing. However, it was too late. The contract was signed, and I began to prepare a handover document for the business unit that would be running the platform. As much as I was annoyed by the limitations, my role, up till then, had only been in aiding in the selection of the technology. Until that changed a couple of weeks before the handover. The vice president of the division called a meeting with my boss and me. He began:

"During this process, as you noticed, Awareness talked about investing in a community person. Now I know you are the marketing manager and have a lot on your plate, but we now need a community manager. Maybe one day we will hire for that, but for now, I'd like you to take that role on. Get the site up and running, create engagement, and once it's successful, we can see about getting a full-time community person to take this on. How does this sound?"

Now I know what you are thinking — "Don't do it, Adrian." Maybe you are even yelling at this point. I was just afraid to say no and let them down. I also felt it really wasn't an ask; it was more of an order. I also knew they *needed* someone. I agreed to be the community manager, on top of my other work, hoping I could do both. I became the accidental B2B community manager.

As I would learn many years later, most people fall into the community role — just like I did. It's not sought. It finds them. Also, I learned quickly, hobby communities are one thing. When it comes to being paid to run a community, it's like being given a Ferrari right after you learn to drive. It's nerve-wracking, exciting, exhilarating, and you shit yourself worrying about wrecking this shiny new car because the power, and all the eyes, are on you. I felt this all at once — as most accidental community managers do.

After the meeting, I went back to my desk, my head spinning, and I began to research "How to build a B2B community." There wasn't much out there at the time. I knew the basics of running a hobby community, but I didn't actually know how to run one for a business. I also didn't know why they were building this community and who the target audience was. When I asked for guidance, I was told to do my best to fill the community with existing blog content. They also asked me to create some conversations amongst a couple of self-created accounts. I created a dozen profiles and filled the community up with questions and answers. I loaded all kinds of documents to support those answers, based on FAQs I found on our website.

My main objective was to get the community ready to present to the business unit, which would ultimately take control of it. Once that was done, the latest plan was that I would manage the platform on the technical side (kind of a precursor to community operations), but day-to-day interactions with customers and content creation would be their responsibility.

Eventually, the community was ready to hand over. My team was happy with the end result. All that was left to do was to meet with the new stakeholders. That would happen a few days later. The training took place in a large conference room with large windows overlooking the city. I began by telling them about the software we chose, how it worked, and a showed them a live demo that was ready to launch, full of content. I looked out over the room of about 15 people when I was done. All I saw were blank stares.

Finally, the head of their team raised a hand.

"Yes, go ahead. I am happy to answer any questions," I said excitedly.

She looked at me over the rim of her glasses. "This isn't what we wanted!"

I was taken aback and shocked, and I promised to share her feedback. After a day or two of meetings, things were finally smoothed out. It was understood this new space could be the hub for partners they wanted, but it could also be used for supporting customers. I was happy to have her finally on board. So, I began to talk about next steps.

"Can I go ahead and create accounts for your engineers?" I asked.

"No. They don't want to use this tool. They get emails. Answering emails is their primary job. If you get a question in the forum, send us an email. We'll answer you, and then you can post it."

Unsuccessfully, I tried to push back and tell her how using the forum directly would be more efficient. She didn't take well to my concerns about how this workflow would add delays. I was also concerned we would not be answering people with an authentic voice. She didn't care — this was not a fight she was willing to have with her technical team. I gave up. I should have taken a different approach, for example, to involve the technical team lead directly or to explain how it would reduce their repetitive workload. But I did not have the knowledge I have now. I also had orders to make it work. Not wanting to rock the boat further, I agreed to her plan.

After a couple of weeks, there was a soft launch with our internal teams. It didn't last more than a couple of days.

What I had planned as a slow rollout became a "get the community out to the public ASAP." Later that week, on a Friday afternoon, an email was sent to thousands of customers to join our community. The weekend was upon us. I shut my computer down and headed home. I did not worry at the time, because I thought a business community would not have a lot of activity over the weekend.

On Monday morning, when I turned on my computer, my Outlook froze. Slowly, my inbox filled with over 1,200 emails. I checked my work voicemail, and I had over 50 unheard messages. Apparently, spam bots had gone crazy over the weekend.

As I was trying to understand what happened, my phone rang. Of course, it was the head of the business unit, who never wanted this solution to start with.

"What the hell happened? All our customers are being spammed. Not to speak of all the spam in the community. You better fix this ASAP."

Then my boss called. "Get on the phone with Awareness ASAP. In the meantime, shut off the site until you fix things."

I started to get angry and frustrated. Mostly because, as I tried to fix things, people kept coming by my desk to ask me if I knew they were being spammed. I found a quiet corner to hide from them. I called up Awareness. The phone rang for what seemed like forever. When they picked up, I tried to remain calm.

"Hey, I am not sure you saw, but we got spam-bombed over the weekend. Do you have anything to prevent spam or any flood controls to prevent so many posts in such a short period by one person?" I asked my contact at Awareness.

"Let me look into this. In the meantime, I will send you an email on how you can set your community to preapproval mode, so no one can simply just join or post to the community."

I put down the phone. I wrote an email to the community, explaining what happened, apologizing to everyone, and outlining what we were doing next. I then began removing all the spam, banning accounts, and turning the community to an approval-only method.

My phone rang shortly after I sent the email.

"Hi, it's George" — not his real name — "from Awareness. Sorry, Adrian, we don't have spam or flood controls as you describe, but we can build them for your company. It will cost about $5,000."

"Wow. Are you sure? Isn't spam checking and flood control kind of a must-have for forums?" I asked.

"Honestly, none of our customers has ever asked us for this, so we'd have to build it for you," replied George.

I was shocked into silence. I hung up the phone and reported the cost to my boss. I waited and then got a predictable answer: "No more budget would be approved." I had to stick with the approval method now enabled.

I tried my best to make the community work. The questions would come into the forum. I would write: "Great question, let me have the engineers look into this." I would forward the email and wait for an answer. Sometimes it would take days, in spite of my following up. Sometimes the engineers would just answer the customer by email directly, finding them in our CRM, and never send me the answer to post in the forum. Eventually, they pivoted the concept of the community, and their marketing manager took over. It never got traction with their audience. I remained as a community administrator, ultimately responsible for the relationship with our vendor, Awareness Networks.

Then, one day, we got a fateful email from them. Awareness was deprecating their forum product to focus on their social tool. Our community experiment came to an end with little fanfare. We decided to sunset the community and not pay for a migration to another tool. A couple of weeks before Awareness shut down, we closed our community. I'm not sure anyone noticed at that point. Within a couple of days, the marketing team proceeded to eradicate the digital footprint of any link or mention to our community. No one would know it had ever existed.

Before I move on from the past, I should be clear. I don't blame anyone. We were in mostly uncharted territories for B2B communities. These were the early days of the community industry. It was certainly before much of the great work and resources the community space has now. I also want to take a lot of blame for not having the confidence to speak with authority. I allowed myself to assume others knew better. However, I learned a lot because of this experience. It also wouldn't be my only failure in building communities — but who's perfect? Thankfully, I have been lucky to also celebrate many successes, fueled by the lessons that failures such as this have taught me.

You may wonder why I gave you all this background on my first paid B2B community. There are a couple of reasons. One, it's to show we all start somewhere. Two, it's to be clear we don't always have the right answers. Three, it's okay to make mistakes, as long as you learn from them and don't make the same ones again. Most importantly, I shared this story because this experience was so formative for me. It's at the forefront of my mind as I write this book. Without these experiences, the book you have in your hands would not exist.

So what happened next in my career? After three more years working in various web marketing roles, I joined Vanilla Forums in 2013. The small start-up I always admired would now benefit from all my experiences over the last 14 years. As I grew in my career with Vanilla, I watched, learned, and helped launch countless thriving communities. Over time, I began to understand my first experience as a paid community builder was not unique. What I lacked was a cheerleader to encourage me to do the right things and to share their secrets on how to do it. My greatest hope is that this book becomes that for you. Oh, and if time travel ever becomes possible, I'll drop a copy on the desk of past me. Let's now go forward and build some great communities together!

Chapter 3: How "Real" Should You Be as a Community Manager?

I am so excited you are entering this adventure. Now begins your first big question, which comes up almost immediately to any community person. Who will you be in the community? Or, more specifically, "How should the community manager be presented in an online community?" You're not the first person to wrestle with this question.

I get it. If you're coming from social media or another marketing role, it could be tempting to consider just presenting yourself as the logo or under the company name in the community. It seems like the logical choice. It may even be what your bosses want.

So, what should you do? I can't tell you what to do. I can only share my advice and what I've seen the most successful communities do. Simply put, every community needs a clearly defined person, or team of people, that is real and present in the space. However, the level of realness depends on several other considerations, such as the community, the topic, and any personal safety concerns the community manager may have.

I would strongly advise you not to interact with your community under a company brand-username, for example, XYZCompany. I'd also advise you to not use your company logo as an avatar. You can create a separate account to post company news or community announcements using the company logo. However, your main community manager account should be undeniably personalized. If you're asking people in your community to connect, share, and be themselves, you yourself need to embody these values. You need to be as authentic as you're going to ask them to be...well, to some extent, of course! Not everything is for public consumption!

In a business community, where people are professionals, you can likely use your real first name and photo with little concern. There's still a risk, however, as with anything on the internet, of unwanted attention. Most experienced community managers are aware of this, which is why no company should ever force anyone to use their real photo or full name. There are also certain types of communities, such as ones where emotions run high (e.g., gaming or crypto communities), where I would never tell someone to use their real full name and photo. But, even without a real name or photo, you can still be *real.* Never lose the human element of who you are.

When I talk about being "real," I mean you should have a clear persona — don't be too shy to share your love of chocolate or dogs. You can use a username that suits the community—maybe a nickname or your middle name. In terms of photos, make sure the image you use in the community is unique to the community. It can be a real photo or even one of your dogs (who doesn't love that?). I would caution you, too, if you want to keep your true identity out of the community, be careful about which photo you choose. It's very easy to reverse search an image on Google to find out who you are. If you use that image elsewhere with your full identity, it's not hard to find out who you are. Yes, I know it's a sad time to be alive, but you need to be aware of your safety too. So, if you have concerns, please take precautions.

I know most never have an issue, and it's likely neither will you — especially in a B2B community. However, I would be remiss not to warn you. I have heard horrific stories from male and female colleagues, mentioning death threats, unwanted attention, doxing (sharing of personal information online), and general creepiness. Certainly, this has skewed mostly towards my friends in the gaming industry. However, I'm aware of a few instances where community builders in the software space (non-gaming) were targeted because a user was not happy with a company decision or were sent unwelcome messages because of their race, sex, gender, or political leaning. While very rare, I think this is a risk you need to know about.

However, before I scare you too deeply, I want to assure you there are settings in most community platforms to filter, block, and assist you in most of these scenarios. We will talk about those in later chapters. For my part, I have always been "Adrian" or "Adrian Speyer" in every business community I have managed. I always use my professional photo, but I also recognize my privilege to do that. Only you can decide your comfort and situation, but in most B2B communities it should not be an issue. Whatever you do or choose, the key is to authentically be yourself. Let your personality shine through. *Be yourself as much as you want and as is appropriate.*

Now that we have a good idea of who you are, let's dive into finding you a home!

Chapter 4: Should We Even Have an Online Forum?

We need talk about the space you build for your community. Your community will exist even if you don't create a spot for them. You don't "permit" people to create an online community. They will naturally congregate into spaces. They will take to Twitter, Reddit, fan forums, or whatever online space makes sense.

I guess this would be as good a place as any to make sure you know exactly what a community is. Your followers are not a community, nor are the people who consume or use your product. A community will have these four elements:

- A shared **space** for people to gather and connect
- People who **share common** language (jargon), customs, interests, or passions
- People who share with one another **voluntarily and among themselves** in this space
- People who feel a **sense of belonging** in this group and have a **genuine** interest in supporting/assisting/sharing/learning from each other

When anyone in your company talks about or used the word "community," we want to make sure they meet this definition. Once it's clear we are talking community, the next question to answer is, *should* you, as a company, be creating a space for your community? Almost always, the answer is yes, but with a caveat: *Don't build an online forum unless you are willing to truly invest in its success!*

Seriously! If you want to waste your time, build a space where no one in the company is willing to spend the time, effort, or money on the project. In my years working with businesses, the ones that succeeded understood that investment is more important than the platform. And once you have the technology, you need to know *why* you are building a forum and what you hope to achieve. This book will dive deeper into this in the coming chapters.

It may have shocked some of you to hear someone working for a forum software company tell you that the platform is not the sole determinant for community success. Indeed, a platform needs to include your must-have features, stability to handle traffic, and security to keep your data safe. From that perspective, platforms do matter. However, it's not the platform that will determine success, it's the extent to which a company is willing to put time, effort, and human resources behind it that is the true determinant for success.

I do want to also talk about technology. There are some platforms that are better than others on which to build your community from a business sense. In this case, serious businesses shouldn't consider making their home on any off-domain platform, such as Reddit or Facebook, as tempting as the word "free" can be. Indeed, these can be supplemental to your cause, but I would caution against making them your central hub for your customers. "Why?" you ask.

These are the following things you need to consider when building a central hub for conversations with your customers:

- Branding
- SEO
- Data access
- Marketing
- Technical know-how

Let's tackle each of these.

First, let's start with a story. Imagine, if you would, your company is hosting a fabulous open house party. Spotlights are out, the band is playing, a red rope and carpet are outside. People are being handed glasses of champagne, and then they are led into a room. Inside the room, there are no decorations. The only snacks are sad trays of crackers with cheese. No music, no personality. This room could be anywhere, at any company. It's nothing special. And you want people to stay? Good luck. I'd leave, and so would you. Don't create a bland space. Make your online community experience the most inviting place on your website. Let's make it a space people just can't wait to get into, because of the value and insight it offers.

Let's take a closer look at community branding. If I am dealing with a premium product or a serious company, I expect a spectacular experience. When I click on that community link on your website, I expect to enter a lovely online community that matches your brand's look and feel. I do not expect to be shuttled to Facebook or a table-based, pathetic, home-brew job with a GeoCities palette of colours. You should spend as much (if not more) time and money on the design and experience of your branded community. It's the space where your customers, and potential customers, will likely come first.

Another aspect of creating an outstanding online forum is SEO (search engine optimization). Think of SEO as an open invitation to attract people to your party. What is SEO, really? It's the art (and some would say science) of creating an online property that Google and other search engines will show high up in search results in a favourable way. When a customer or potential customer has an issue, a search engine is where they start. What do you want to happen when your potential customers ask a question within your domain? Don't you want your online

31

community to have the answer? Do you really want to send them to your social network page or an online property you control? Think of all the great information you're giving away when they don't come to you. Think of all the information you're giving to that network's advertisers and your potential competitors. If you don't focus on SEO, you'll miss the opportunity to solve problems for countless potential community members looking for a solution you can offer.

Let's go deeper into my comment about giving away your information for free on these other spaces. Imagine, if you would, at this open house party at your company, you could not see the invitation list beyond a name. Let's be even more precise. You can only know the name people put on their badges. You don't know their real name, where they work, why they came, how they found you, or even a way to reach them after the party. They could even be *lying* about who they are. They could be a competitor, snarfing down a cheese plate and drinking all your wine, while stealing your customers.

This is no different from the content you are giving away on those spaces you don't own. Sure, members on these non-owned platforms give you information, but do they give you the critical information? What percentage of users come from mobile? How long did they look at the content? Did they consume any offers from the page? What kind of content are people searching for? Are they currently a customer?

When you don't own the platform, you don't own the data. You are making business decisions based on the data the platform *decides* to give you. The best info is kept for them and for marketing their own products — or advertising. I've done social media marketing for a dozen years, and all the data I ever saw was for targeting ads to audience. I hardly got consumption metrics. Frankly, most of these platforms never give anything beyond vanity metrics, despite all the efforts many people have made in building up these platform "for free." Worst of all, these platforms still control the communications to your customers. If you build on these networks, eventually they will make you pay to contact your own customers. What a great idea! Charging us to contact those who had already indicated interest by following our pages. They *wanted* to hear from us, and now we needed to pay to speak to them!

Early on, people would brag about having over one million followers on Facebook. However, what always mattered was what percentage of those they could actually reach. Facebook controls that. Can you email those one million people when you need to, without paying? Forget that. What about the one person saying nasty things about you on your Instagram? Can you even confirm they are a paying customer? Kind of hard to do, with only a screen name, and no sales data or email info. And yet, somehow, businesses are choosing to use these platforms as their primary connection spot. Notice how many websites push their social media and hide their branded community. Let be clear, though, I am not saying you shouldn't build on Facebook or Instagram; I am saying don't make it more prominent than your own branded community. Your business would never just hand over its customer list to a third party, so why would you not control the list of your most passionate fans and advocates?

Another pitfall of being on a platform you don't control is that it's counter to one of the actual goals of marketing. Marketing's goal is about moving prospects along the buyer's journey towards purchase. A social network will allow others to advertise next to your page. Going back to our open house at your company metaphor, imagine, if you will, as people are walking towards your party, they see offers for a better party? Maybe free drinks? A lower-cost option? Not only do they see these ads, but they're also on your property, right in their face, all the way to the door. Why would you allow this?

One more thought about marketing. The most valuable thing your marketing team has is an email. It allows you to tie, to great detail, a person's behaviour on your digital properties. It enables you to make offers to them, connect with them, or reach out if there is a problem . . . and, guess what, you don't have access to this for anyone not on your *own* platform. Does it make sense to be at such a disadvantage?

Even beyond marketing, your customer success and experience teams want to have more control. They want to build amazing experiences along the customer journey towards value realization, and ultimately renewal, and even upsell. Good luck with that without access to the actual platform to make it happen.

With hope, after all of this, you see that owning your platform is the way to go. However, let me caution you before you develop your own in-house solution rather than go with a hosted platform. Let's return to a party example. To plan a party is easy. We all have, at some point, entertained friends at our place or a restaurant. However, it's a bit more complicated when we consider something more extensive, like a wedding. We may take a year to plan, have some help — maybe even the venue has a coordinator. I mean, there is a reason many call it "the big day."

Nonetheless, you could still go it alone if you choose or if you don't have the budget. Besides, it's only a hundred people (or less), and they're related to you and love you. You have a home-court advantage. Most will likely be forgiving if things are not perfect — at least, I hope so.

Now imagine a party where you expect thousands, or hundreds of thousands, of people. Some like you already, and others will need you to make a good first impression. Do you have the necessary skills? I mean, surely you could try, but your job and skills are not likely to create events at that scale. Do you know what to expect? Are you able to coordinate so many moving parts alone? What about a backup plan if things go sideways?

Consider your community platform as your big party. Thousands will come. They expect flawless execution. Your company has customers who pay for your product or service. Your brand and reputation are something so important that failure can be costly. Can you trust your company developers with such a project? Why would you ever try to place your platform in the hands of someone without experience? This goes from building your own custom community platform, to figuring out how to handle a surge of web traffic, security against hackers, file hosting, device compatibility, and more.

Let's say you decide to do it in-house. What happens when your technical team gets pushed to another more important project (it will happen) or the person who knows your in-house platform leaves the company (this will happen too). I think this is one of the main reasons people opt for Facebook, Reddit, or other free platforms. However, in trying to avoid using the internal developers or buying a hosted platform, you actually lose money and opportunities for your business — including access to your own business data.

It's not all doom and gloom. Let me stop to provide something for the benefit of my friends who actually work at Reddit, LinkedIn, and Facebook. Let me be clear — these are fine platforms. People will still use them, and I am not suggesting you stop. They are great avenues for awareness and brand discovery. However, I do suggest the primary spot to place your energy should be on your own domain — in your own branded community. You can still promote or build on these other channels, but you need to go with your eyes open. Spending time building long term on rented land may not make sense when the landlord can evict you or change the lease at any time without your consent. I like to use social channels as teasers to entice people to come to my owned branded community, rather than build solely on these social spaces. I know another reason many companies opt for building on these networks. It feels much easier to build on social for most marketers, because they understand it. However, I can't caution your enough, if your brand matters, guard against making it your primary channel.

That's not to say social networks don't have some benefits. Using social can be a great way to gauge interest in your community concept. It's a low-cost and easy way to get going too. However, don't stay on them as your primary spot long-term. In my experience, these networks eventually fail when scaling to accommodate a larger community, and then companies are stuck trying to make a hard transition. So, if you start on social, always have an exit strategy — and leave before inertia makes it more difficult. Be ready to pivot your social strategy to be the entrance to your party, not the destination.

At this point, I hope I've convinced you to choose a good, hosted platform for your business community. Easy, right? Well, I am not so naive as to think that. There are so many platforms out there to choose from. How to decide? I mean, I know what my choice would be, but I understand company politics and restrictions. Recall my earlier story? Sadly, I know I'm not alone.

One community builder I met, told me they could choose between two platforms, per her internal company process. Her two choices were Jive or Lithium. Well, guess what? Eventually, Jive was bought by Lithium. She only had one choice, which was to migrate from Jive to Lithium. She was stuck, even though the platform lacked the features she needed to be successful. That was, until she convinced them to add an alternative. I was so excited when they launched on Vanilla. The stakes were huge for their company and their millions of members. Making the wrong choice could be career-ending. However, as of this writing, she made the right choice, the community is thriving, and she got promoted to head of a department.

Sometimes, as the accidental community manager, you have no choice. One of these three fates is very common: Use an existing solution which may or may not be best, choose a new platform ASAP with a ridiculous timeline, or inherit a platform you never selected in mid-migration. There is a fourth fate, where you are given the ability and time to choose a platform or have significant input. I hope this is your fate.

Too many times I have seen forums moved to another platform, which killed their branded community. There were bugs so severe that the platform was unusable or promises made by the vendor regarding data migration were not kept. Thankfully, I have only been a witness to these other platform failures — never involved — but it's still heartbreaking nonetheless.

I think what makes it the most difficult is that you know it could be avoided. The community doesn't die, it's just the space the brand created which is destroyed. The community will scatter to other places. Good luck when this brand tries to recreate the community once a trust is broken. So, if you have any say in platform selection, it's worth fighting, taking the time, and making sure you do it right . . . with a plan.

In my first experience of choosing the wrong platform, I was not alone. I did not take the sole blame for its failure. Also, it was a new community, so we didn't have the extra pressure of betraying or alienating our established community by our mistakes. Nonetheless, any time a community fails, it leaves scars. Not only did it leave a lasting impression on me, almost 10 years later the company had still not attempted another community. No one in management had the appetite, because it was seen as a failure. However, I think what hurts most is that our company's competitor got it right, eventually. We approached it the wrong way, with no proper plan, no buy-in of key stakeholders, and a really flawed community platform. As I write this chapter, all I can think about is how I can help you avoid a similar outcome.

Our team's problem in the selection phase was this: We didn't know what to ask, and we didn't know what we should have known. So, for your benefit, if ever you have to choose a platform, here is what you need to consider and what to ask. You should feel comfortable with the answers you're given and walk away if you don't. Consider these "must-ask" questions. Indeed, there will be other requirements for your stakeholders, but these should help cover the most basic requirements (and, time machine friends, once again, please pass this to my former self):

Can I Customize the Look?

I made it clear earlier: if you are serious about your brand (and who isn't?), you will want a solution that can do more than allow you to add your logo and change the background colour. You want the community to look and feel exactly like the rest of your website. You need to understand how, and if, you can control these changes yourself. It's also important to know if you are stuck on your vendor's timeline or you can make changes on the fly — with or without being an experienced developer. Finally, you need to consider if you need to secure design help or pay for professional services.

Is It Easy to Administer, Moderate, and Use?

Administering your community should be easy, intuitive, and not be a huge drain on your time. Several hundred-page user manuals should not be needed. It's also great to have tons of control pages, but also remember, with greater complexity, can come more issues and problems. What if you need someone to step in because of a vacation? Will they be overwhelmed? What kind of training will you get? Is it extra?

Also, from a user perspective, is it easy to use, or will it require a significant learning curve? Is it mobile-friendly? Can people login in with social media credentials or current company/account credentials? Let's not put friction into adoption and another password to recall.

How Is It Hosted?

Ask about how it's hosted. Where is the hardware located? What kind of security does it have? Is there a disaster plan or redundancy in place for a worst-case scenario? This is where even I, an optimist, will warn you to think about what could happen. What happens if the data centre's location has a power blackout, flood, mudslide, fire, earthquake, or tornado? What is the plan, so your community does not go down? Do you want a software as a service (SaaS) solution, or do you want to self-host? Self-hosting might look less expensive, but the total cost of ownership (setup, licenses, maintenance, etc.) can add up. A

SaaS solution means little to no IT hassles and easy setup, but it also means finding a vendor you can trust and that you want to work with over the long run. SaaS, to me, is a no-brainer, only because I have seen what happens long term for self-hosted solutions. You will have to decide whether your company will, indeed, be committed to forum upkeep. Most times, self-hosted works well short term — until a browser manufacturer makes a change that breaks things, or the IT team that builds your software moves onto the next project. You need to be mindful of what happens when the software requires a bug fix or an update, and who exactly will help. The beauty of SaaS is that one of the critical aspects you pay for is peace of mind.

What Is the Support Model?

Just like insurance, the quality of support is essential when bad things happen, and you need it most. You might also need development support if you plan on creating close integrations between your community and your website or other systems and those skills don't exist in-house. Or maybe you have a dev, but they need a technical contact to point them in the right direction. Know what you have and what you may need, by scoping out the project for now and the future. Also, read the contract carefully. Understand what kind of support you get and how you get it. Do you have a phone number to call? Is there a service-level agreement (SLA) regarding how fast they get back to you? Is there a penalty for them if there is downtime? Where is it your responsibility to customize, and where can they help? For example, if a vendor allows you to build custom themes, and your dev deploys sloppy code that takes down the site, does the vendor troubleshoot it?

If nothing else is recalled from this bit, it brings me back to the earlier point of having the right people with the right technical skills in your company. What gaps will need to be filled, either through the vendor or hiring someone before starting your project? Please don't assume. This is especially true when it comes to integration. A vendor does not want to troubleshoot the working of another software they don't make. It doesn't matter how ubiquitous WordPress

or Google Analytics is; they will not be able to troubleshoot your setup extensively. Hence, trial run due diligence is so crucial to avoid any disappointments.

How Is the Software Upgraded?

Most times, when a forum or community is hacked, it's because the owner was using old software that was not updated. Ask your potential vendor: how are upgrades handled for the software? Are they included in the cost? How hard is it to upgrade? Some vendors might require you to pay an upgrade fee to be on the latest version of the software. Others may require downtime. The best make it hardly noticeable. Ensure you get release notes and a staging area before it's pushed to production. Ahh, staging area, which of course, means...

Do You Get a Developer or Staging Area?

One of the golden rules of website building is to never test on a live site. You'll want to have a staging environment. This means a copy of your community only you and your team can use, to try things out before they get pushed live. This is a place to test upgrades before they go live, to test features, or even simply how a new image or a tweak to your CSS will make your community look. What happens when you turn on a new feature? Test it first. Don't go live without some safety net.

Do I Own 100 Percent of My Data?

Sometimes things don't work out, and you need to change community providers. If you are self-hosted, it's pretty easy to get to your data. If you choose hosted or SaaS, be very careful about who you choose. Some hosted solutions do not allow you to take your data with you, or make it very difficult. Do not become a hostage to your vendor. Ask about this before you sign the contract, and make sure the contract has clear language about what happens with your data should you need it. Also, make sure it's in a format you can use. If they give you an export in a format that can only be opened by their proprietary software, it's kind of useless. They might as well print it out and send it to you in the mail.

How Easy Is It to Configure and Integrate?

Will configuration require a professional services engagement? What will that cost? Is the product extensible via well-documented APIs, to let your developers integrate it into your other systems? What are the systems you need to have integrated — must-have vs. nice-to-have? This has come up in my points above, but it just shows you how precise you need to be with what is meant by "technical assistance." Don't just say you need an integration with a community provider; they will always say yes. Be specific as to what you mean by "integrate."

Does It Have All the "Must-Have" Features?

Ensure you scope out the must-have features you want for your community before you sign up (and before you get frustrated by the limitations). Remember how we bought a platform without spam or flood control? I assumed this was standard. Don't assume.

Here are some common features to ask about:

42

- Can we control who joins? For example, can you make is so only customers can join?
- Can we have public and private spaces?
- How extensive is the API? What are the limitations? How detailed is your documentation?
- Does it have single sign-on (which lets users connect with your current authentication system)?
- Can we restrict member permissions to only view specific categories?
- Can users upload files? Can we control that?
- How does it handle multiple languages?
- Can we sync information to our CRM? Is it a one-way or two-way sync?
- How is the community protected from spam/bots?
- What kind of analytics are included? What format do they come in? Can we export it?
- Tell us about hosting? Security? Disaster plan? Recovery? Backups?
- Is gamification and ideation included or extra?

Can You Trust the Platform's Creator?

If your community is critical to your success (it is, isn't it?), you will also want to look deeper at the creator of the software. Are they trustworthy? Do they have a team that stands behind the product? Who is on their team? Do they regularly release updates and new features, and are they still innovating? Do other brands you recognize use them (or *still* use them)? Can you talk to their customers? What do the review sites say? What do other community managers think of the platform? The community forum software space is full of options and opinions. Take your time and read contracts carefully. Don't risk your company reputation on experimental, unproven, or soon-to-be deprecated software.

How Much Time Do I Need?

Please, please, please plan . . . and then work backwards. Are you weeks away from a significant event in Q4? Sorry, but you will likely need to go with the bare minimum or consider that your community launch may need to be your next event. Yes, you can have something up in a day — heck, hours in the digital world — but having it done appropriately takes time. Don't rush things. It's like poached eggs in the microwave. Sure, you can have poached eggs in under one minute, but the best ones made traditionally with the appropriate amount of time, will always be beyond comparison. If your first experience is microwaved poached eggs, you'll likely think they are a horrible mess, and you'll never want them again. Don't be the person cutting corners. Take time to show your community you care about the little things. If you're asking them to spend their time there, the least you can do is put your best effort forward.

Phew, that was a long list, but essential. I would not *ever* buy a community platform without being happy with the answers to the above questions, and neither should you. Certainly, this is not an exhaustive list, and much of it depends on your needs, but I think it's a solid starting point.

As someone who has bought software at the enterprise level, remember, some vendors may have salespeople who say yes, even when things are not 100 percent exactly to your needs. Make extra sure your critical items are in the package, and at a price that won't come with extra surprise later. Push for a demo instance to try things out. Bring in all the stakeholders for the process. Bring in the teams that will interface daily with the platform so they can be part of the process, catch inconsistencies, and participate in giving their opinion. I know it's not always possible but having them involved works better than imposing a solution after the fact. They may even offer you good questions or "gotchas" to look for before you sign on the dotted line.

One final thought on buying platforms. I want to give you a final warning about choosing the right solution for the problem. No one wants to hammer nails with a butter knife. Maybe you are already stuck with a technology albatross. Sometimes a suite your company uses already offers a community component, but it's just bare bones. Don't fall for discount community. Ask the questions above. Sometimes companies try to make their CMS platform into a community platform via a plugin. For example, they will try to turn Drupal, Joomla, or WordPress into an online community. Before it's too late and you realize it's missing core functionality for your needs, so make sure you ask the questions above.

I know you may be blocked from investing in a proper tool by your organization. Hopefully, you win the battle and get the ability to buy or migrate to a suitable platform. Maybe showing them this book will help. It's a fight worth having. Don't try to make use of a solution beyond its core competency. It's like ordering fried chicken from a pizzeria. Certainly, it's possible, but likely not very good. A friend of mine learned this hard way after getting food poisoning. Don't let that be you.

I hope this chapter gives you the fundamentals to get the right platform. Let's now get started with building your community.

Chapter 5: The MVP: The Core Principle

What are the main reasons brand communities fail? There are a few. Most times, it comes down to not proving impact to stakeholders or lack of a solid plan to connect with this potential audience you want to build a community for.

In thinking about this, I wondered if I could come up with a repeatable recipe to help community builders. I begin building community with a simple principle. Don't think about *users*. Don't think about *community members*. Clear your mind of everything, and only think about *people*. Communities are always about people. I know it sounds obvious, but it's amazing how often a community is built without thinking about that fact.

People have other things to worry about than your community. At the same time, people can create massive change when they come together. You want your online community to be *their* space. If you are coming from the marketing space, to truly make a successful community, you need to stop seeing members as leads or prospects. Your boss can tell you what *they* want, using whatever term they want. But, as the champion of the people of your online community, don't forget who actually populates this space.

It may take a while to learn this, but trust me, as you start meeting people from your online community individually (either on calls or in-person), it will get easier to apply this. You need them in your mind's eye when you consider how to build your community. However, until this happens, you'll be stuck in the "fake it until you make it" mode. Just follow me for a bit more.

Every community I have ever worked on that was an absolute success followed a "people-first" philosophy even if they didn't realize it. By reading this book, you will go down the path of doing this *consciously*.

The concept is what I call the "MVP principle." It is the fundamental foundation that guides me in all the community-building I do. Now some people see MVP and think "minimal viable product," but, for our purposes, the MVP principle is about "most valuable people." There is a slight twist, though. I think most valuable people exists with a duality — both external and internal MVPs. Don't worry, I'll explain more below.

External MVP

Building a successful community starts, as I mentioned above, with the recognition that a community is made of people, and by focusing on putting their needs first. Your end goal,
or what you want to achieve, is to create an army of most valuable people, connecting them to a place that matters, is of consequence, and is a space they care for. We want to build a space where people feel connected to the community and who become advocates on your behalf.

As a community manager, your external task will be to identify, encourage, and support these advocates. Empower these people to be leaders, so when you and your team can't be online, you don't need to worry. You want to make them feel special. You can do this by sharing insider knowledge, granting special privileges or access, or through recognition.

Doing this thoughtfully will allow you to create a group that can help create content, onboard others into your community, and ensure your other customers or clients have a rewarding experience.

If nothing else, please remember you shouldn't tell people how *you* want your community to be. You should ask what they need from the community to be successful at their goals, and then take their input and work to create a space that helps them achieve those outcomes. Too many businesses make assumptions, or put business goals first, without actually talking to the real people who will make up the community. As a community manager, make those connections and have those conversations. Bring the needs of real people to the planning and building of your community.

I would like to leave you, also, with a word of caution, as someone who has done this a lot. You want to get a sense of your audience motivation, however, what people *tell* you is not the only thing to act on. It's a datapoint to add to your research. I would combine this with observing what these people do in other spaces and what their interactions are naturally, so you have a more holistic view.

Internal MVP

Just as we focus on people we care about externally, this should continue when it comes to the people within your company and your internal MVPs — or as some call them, stakeholders. As a matter of fact, this is the most essential aspect of the MVP principle. The true measurement of success for your community (and the security of your employment) requires organizational success. You need to identify the most valuable people in your company and make the community a vital hub for the company. Think of them as "core stakeholders" to your success. These are the people who can secure you more budget, assist you in getting more resources, and champion the work you do to other executives. The higher up in the company you can go, the better.

You want to focus on the goals (KPIs) that matter to these MVPs within your business and ensure your community strategy aligns to these goals. You can also measure anything you like in your community, but be strategic in what you report up. Your stakeholder reports should connect community activity to your core business objectives.

How to know what those are? This is where the people-centric portion of planning comes in. You need to have a conversation with your management, or hopefully, you already know the core objectives of your stakeholders. You now want to correlate the two. Always try to tie one metric to an outcome per stakeholder. If you don't have an outcome directly linked to the company's success, your KPI is not solid enough, and you may need to rethink what you've selected.

For example, every boss wants more revenue, but how will you measure this with the community? Maybe it's a measure of how much community content leads to the sign-up page? Maybe the goal is to reduce churn. Maybe you notice that people who find content more helpful in the community rate you higher in satisfaction surveys. Happy customers churn less. For your product stakeholder, measure how many new ideas from the community get into the final product.

The main thing to remember is a community is part of an overall digital strategy . . . or it should be. This means there should be analytics on your community and across your digital properties. You need to have a holistic view to do your best to tell the impact of your work. Please don't think you need to become an analytics expert overnight.

Most companies have someone who can help you. You just need to direct them to the questions you need answered.

I also realize that getting to this information varies significantly, depending on your company, but it's worth the time. I can promise you, not having this conversation is a ticking time bomb. One day, when you don't expect it, someone will question the value of what you do or why your community exists. Be ahead of the curve and start the conversation as soon as possible.

I know this is a distasteful concept for some, but your career and community success depend on this. You can measure whatever you need for community health, sense of community, and other measurements. However, I can't overstate this enough. When you report to management how your community is doing, report only the KPIs that matter to your business goals and those stakeholders you care about. Don't be ashamed to tell them how your community helps. Don't assume they know. Don't think they will figure it out. Tell them and tell them regularly. If you're shy, do it by email, but do it.

Why am I so insistent on this? I want you to win. And I want to make you sure your community is seen as an important hub for the business. I want you to shout from the rooftops so they know you are a vital part of the team. You need to not only tell them, but show them that the community is seen as core to its success. If you, as the community manager, could quit tomorrow, and the business would go on, you need to figure out how to change that. Think how the community can be the centre for product feedback, product ideas, product innovation, reducing support, creating content, driving leads, or helping sales close deals.

There is an upside to creating this value for the company, as well. When you align the community's activities to be an essential source for achieving company goals it makes it easier for them to understand what you're trying to do. In its simplest form you are trying to make the company succeed and you're trying to make the stakeholders look good. With a solid plan you'll be able to secure commitments for additional resources to be successful. What kind of commitment? It could be something as simple as having the CEO do an AMA (ask me anything), gaining access to product management, getting more budget for swag, adding people to your team, and more.

Personally, I don't know any department head that will say no to any modest request if your community is driving value for the corporation.

Contradictions and Next Steps

I think you probably agree with most of what I shared above, but I know some of you are saying, "Adrian, how can you say a community is about people on the one hand, and then, on the other hand, use the community in such a cold-hearted way to drive KPIs for the business?" Good question. To me, this is the quintessential skill of a fantastic community manager. Your role is to act as an arbitrator of balance, who maximizes both sides, while minimizing the negative for the people who matter.

The job of a community manager is to balance what people care about, in order to encourage them to participate actively in a community, and match them to a company's objectives. Or it could be, in some cases, to find objectives that your company may consider necessary. For example, you may find your community tells you they really want a space to share how others use your product. Your company objective could be to measure customer satisfaction. You could then look at how the community can have an impact on this. The following is a chart to help inspire you.

Department	What Your Boss Cares About	What Your Community Members Care About	Business Outcome
Support	Ticket deflection	Space to share knowledge, help others	Reduce cost to serve
Customer Success	NRR (net revenue retention)	Sense of community, value in connection and access	Increase NPS * (Net Promoter Score®) – How likely people are to recommend you, your company or product (loyalty = less likely to churn)
Product	Product feedback/ ideas	Space to share ideas for better product, early access. Learn how to use the product	CSAT (customer satisfaction score) improvement – which measures customer satisfaction with a business, purchase, or interaction. Usually out of 10
Marketing	Brand awareness	Place to learn from others, or be recognized as an expert	Number of advocacy activities
Sales	Opportunities for prospects, upsells, and upgrades	Get questions answered before purchase	Net revenue increase

I should be clear that, in your company, things might be different. I just wanted to share with you the thought process I go through. Maybe your marketing team cares about leads, so your focus is a collaborative e-book from your community, which becomes a lead magnet elsewhere.

As the community manager, you facilitate the bridge between the two. You are the translator. You are not approaching the community to tell them, "Hey, we want you to buy more and be happy." The message externally is, "Share what you build, inspire, and be inspired." Maybe you have a reward or something that recognizes these fantastic people and their creations. In the end, if you follow my MVP principle, you will have a solid foundation for whatever community you build. As you move through this book, please keep this people-centric mindset. It will be essential as we move forward in building your community plan.

Chapter 6: If It's All About People, It's Also All About the Persona

Up to now, I've written a lot about the importance of people when building a community — so you knew a discussion about personas had to come at some point. Let's dive into understanding personas before we proceed to any content creation or planning. Knowing your personas is crucial to any content endeavour — it can also impact your community plans, workflows, and journeys.

First, let's start off with this: What is a persona? A persona is an archetype, a fictional person you create, based on your data about the people in your current audience or those you hope to attract. It starts with building these profiles around age, gender, and educational background, and should include their fears, challenges, things they care about, and hope to achieve, among other things.

Most companies of any significant size will have these already created. They may live in your sales or marketing organization, and hopefully, they will kindly share them with you. I also know some community experts suggest you create your own personas for the community, but I strongly advise you to blend the two. Why? I think it's better to work with what your company has identified already and overlay how those specific personas would interact with the community. I also think it's perfectly fine to create your own community personas, but I try not to create these in a vacuum. It's possible your marketing personas may not fit into your community personas exactly, so you may need to tweak — but try to keep close to them. These personas are the way all the messaging from your marketing will be to your customers. Knowing this will allow you to be more effective in alignment with other teams.

But what if your company does not have persona profiles? I've been there too. Be the hero and suggest you create some and get involved in it. I would engage the marketing team to assist you, because having a more complete persona will help their work too. Thankfully, there are many great templates online to help you in the process.

Okay, okay, I hear some of you now saying, "All good to tell me to do this, but, Adrian, I don't know how these personas will interact with my community. How can I know?" Well, let's be straight and cut through the marketing bullshit. Most companies create personas without talking to actual people. Marketing makes some educated guesses. Usually, they base it on certain people in the company, or whatever a senior leadership thinks the persona should be. More mature companies will thankfully do this the right way. Don't fret, though, because no matter what you get, you own the community and you have freedom to do it the right way. I like to base the community personas on interactions with real people *actually* in the community. Find the people in your community with similar job titles and seniority as the personas you've been given and make them full formed community personas.

What if you don't have a community or even personas to start with? Ask your marketing team to break down the customer base by title (and seniority, if they can) and make some large buckets. Get access to, or ask for help to, look at your analytics tools. For example, Google Analytics can give you some great insight into age/gender data if it's enabled. Your CRM can give you ideas on job titles, and if your business is about revenue/subscription, you can segment on those successful customers and then use a word cloud to have the titles and experience levels come to the top. You can also leverage your customer success team to help identify potential future members to talk to.

Once you have people and potential segments, what should you do? Interview and talk to people in each identified segment. Here are some persona interview questions:

- Describe your personal situation: Are you married? Do you have kids? Do you live in the city or the suburbs?
- What is your educational background and career path?
- Tell me about your company: What industries do you serve? How big is your company and how many employees do you have, etc.?
- What do you do? Job title and responsibilities? Whom do you report to? Who reports to you?
- What do you care about in your role?
- What are your business goals? What are you measured on?
- What does a typical day look like?
- Which skills are required to do your job?
- What knowledge and which tools do you use in your job?
- What are your most significant work challenges?
- What are your personal business goals?
- What could help you be more successful in your job? What does it mean to be successful in your role?
- How do you learn about new information for your job?
- Which books, magazines, or blogs do you read?
- Which associations, groups, or social networks do you participate in?

- What motivates you to participate?
- How do you feel about sharing your knowledge with others?
- How would you describe your knowledge of our brand, product, or service?
- Who do you think our audience is?
- How do you envision yourself participating in our online community?
- What are things that would be important for us to think about in our community?
- What kind of content would you like to see?
- What kind of community conversations would most interest you?
- What are some examples of great communities you currently participate in? What makes them so great?

This certainly isn't a complete list, but it will help you get started. After these interviews with your target audience or community members, you should be able to build some solid personas. As you do your community content planning, these personas can inform you much better regarding who you are building this space for and the experiences you want them to have.

It may also help you clarify your concept of who your community is for . . . and not for. A community that you will market as a concept based on *experts*, should probably not have a focus on *novice* content. It should start with assumptions on experience level and offer some aspirational goals of advancing those skills. We will get deeper into community content planning in later chapters, but for now, you have a good solid foundation of data to work with.

Chapter 7: Community Discovery and SPAN

You might find that parts of this chapter don't apply to your situation, so skip down to the SPAN portion. I wrote the first portion of this chapter for the community manager dumped into their first project, who has to start from scratch, or who is now leading an *existing* community, especially one they have limited historical knowledge of. The main goal of this chapter is to begin the work of identifying the community you want to build or currently have. Before we delve into any analysis, let's determine if you actually have a "community" or an "audience."

A community exists when people of a like-minded, shared cause, passion, and purpose, are connected to a virtual or physical space where they can connect with others in a symbiotic way. The crucial difference between a community and an audience will be the relationship of giving and taking, not only between the host and members, but also between members around this communal goal. Audiences are not always these multi-faceted interactions. Community is between you, them and their interaction with one another.

This means a community can exist anywhere, truthfully, regardless of whether you use an online platform. You could just be a group of people who tailgate outside the game and love BBQ, but the key is supporting those new to the pastime, and there is some sort of reciprocal relationship. However, it could also be a B2B community for a SaaS company that sells an analytics platform, where people are sharing their tips and tricks, career advice, and connecting with one another. You as a

B2B community manager might not even be involved beyond being a facilitator.

Since there are so many different types of communities, I don't know what kind of situation you will walk into. Maybe you'll be lucky to have this wonderful caring community nucleus to work with, which will require you to observe before you serve. If you're asked to create a community from scratch, you may be stuck with a vast void of no one. This is a much harder proposition — but keep reading I'll give you some tips on that too!

This is where your time as "Sherlock Holmes of Community" comes in. It's time to do the hard work of community discovery. You'll want to get situational awareness of your existing project or what you are taking on.

This is a precursor to any plan. You can't make a community plan until you understand what you are working with. You'll want to get certain questions answered and have a grasp on them before moving to any planning stage. Take your time to get the info you need and meet with the people in your organization who you think can help answer them.

Here are the kinds of questions I like to ask before I start any community project:

What do my own coworkers know? It's a good practice in any company, especially if you come from the outside, to learn if anyone has attempted to create a community before. What worked? What didn't? Can any of these people help?

Where does your community hangout now? You may be creating a space for your community, but they are likely already self-formed elsewhere. We don't make a community, so much as it just exists. We hope our own platform will add an easier way for our organization to interact with them. Find the spaces they are in and seek to get a handle on the topics they care about.

Who are potential community members? Can you identify people in these other communities, who could join your space? Can you work with those other community owners in a respectful and mutually beneficial way? Maybe your Customer Success Manager (CSM), success or sales team can assist in connecting you with the eager and the willing? Check your marketing automation and look for the people consuming your content the most.

Why do they, or would they, participate? Once you identify those spaces and people, talk to them. Find out what matters to them. Really delve into the challenges they face and ways they could do better work. What are the things they like or dislike about your company? No promises here, just fact-finding. Make sure you link back to your personas and validate any assumptions.

Where does your community sit in your organization? Are you reporting to marketing? Are you reporting to support? What are the departmental business goals? How can you impact them with your work? It's important to know who your bosses are and the potential *internal* MVP (most valuable people) you need to impress with the impact of your community work (more on goals in a moment).

Is your company invested in the community? Do they genuinely care about your success? Will you get training? Will you get support from key executives? Are you full time, or are you just doing community part time? These are things that need to be clear when you create a plan. Community is a full-time job in most cases, so you need to be clear about that. You may determine that the community project just doesn't make sense if no one cares to see it succeed.

What are the key goals and objectives for the community? In other words, do you have a clear understanding of why you are in this role and what is expected of you? Not sure? You need to ask. It's hard to plan without knowing what you are planning for. You can use the visualization trick I always use: Ask your management to describe what success with the community would look like? Make sure they don't just *say* "engagement." Get them to define what that means. If you do get KPI, make sure it has some depth and impact. For example, you may start with a KPI regarding the number of discussions and comments, but this is a poor KPI without something more. Be more specific, like determining the number of conversations people found helpful during a specific time interval (e.g., monthly). This could be a measurement of effectiveness and value of content.

What are other technologies in use? Do you have an email platform you can use for newsletters? Do you have a marketing automation platform you can use for segmenting the people of your community? Will you have access to these tools, or are you on your own? If you don't know already, you'll want to understand how you currently engage with your community of customers. Do they get bombarded by newsletters? Maybe adding a separate community newsletter is not a good idea. Is there a way to get that content added to an existing newsletter? Also, if your company is using marketing automation, can your marketing team also create triggers for community members? For example, your marketing automation can be configured to email community members who may not have visited in a while, or it can be used to tell you the kind of content a segment of your community may find interesting.

Is this a multilingual community? Will you have to interface with people in different languages? Maybe ones you don't speak? What kind of support will you have? Also, recall that it's more than translating to the local language; each region has its own customs and practices, which you'll want to ensure you are aware of. It's more about culture and less about language.

What internal/external resources exist? Do you know who you can rely on for help with the community? Who is the product expert in the company? Is there anyone already engaged with the community? Are there natural brand advocates your company has identified? What do they do with them? Are there any current programs taking advantage of internal/external skills? Can you leverage these existing programs for community content, community support, or building your own community plan? This is the time to make friends in other departments. Understand the lingo, the motivators, and who you can rely on or not. This is crucial to building your plan, as you need to have buy-in from these groups to ensure people see value in your community project.

Can you secure an analytics baseline? What does the traffic look like today? Where are you starting from? It's a good idea to create a baseline to see if your efforts have any impact. This does not need to just be Google Analytics. It could be the number of support tickets. It could be the number of product ideas customers email in. Anything, really, that you hope to focus on with your community. The point here is to know about your impact. If you can't show your manager how you moved the needle, consider realigning your goals and objectives to something measurable.

You've done the work and filled a notebook. Keep those notes. We will begin the process of shaping them into something useful, and this starts with *why does or why should the online community exist?* Besides being told the company needs a community, do you clearly understand why the online community should exist? Is it to support your customer? Is it to create better products? What have you learned in your research?

In all my years of community-building, I always see so much excitement at the beginning. It's unfocused energy to do all these fantastic programs and tackle all the needs at once. I used to be the same way. I want you to stay focused. For this purpose, I created the SPAN (Support, Product, Ambassador, Network) framework. It helps to define what kind of community you're trying to build. The concept is based on the fact that most B2B communities will fall into one of four quadrants. Try to situate yourself in one:

Support: The online community will be a member space for self-support and for the company to provide support to their customers. The main goal is reducing support costs by doing more with less and through ticket deflection. It usually involves a question-and-answer feature, and likely integrates with a knowledge base and ticketing system.

Product: The online community is a space for people to share feedback on products and ideas to create better products. Your product management and product marketing teams will be the primary departments you'll want to work with. The focus is product suggestions, identifying and solving common issues, as well as making better products. The content is around guides and people showcasing how they use the product.

Ambassador: The online community primarily focuses on MVPs (most valuable people), who will go out into the world and be your brand loyalists. The goal is to organize and connect with your most passionate fans. It is the ultimate focus group, with thought-provoking discussions between your team and the most ardent users of your product or service. Access for them is key (private beta, insider knowledge, etc.), and in return, they provide crucial feedback. It is not meant to be an open-to-everyone community — only the select ambassadors get in.

Network: This type of community is mainly about networking. The focus is connection among members around a purpose, a cause or a situation –- such as a non-profit. Network communities include communities where value or quality of connection is the main goal – using a member directory, a mentorship program or small community led user groups. This can be mature partner or communities of practice. In essences these are spaces focused on creating bonds — and less about transactional business objectives.

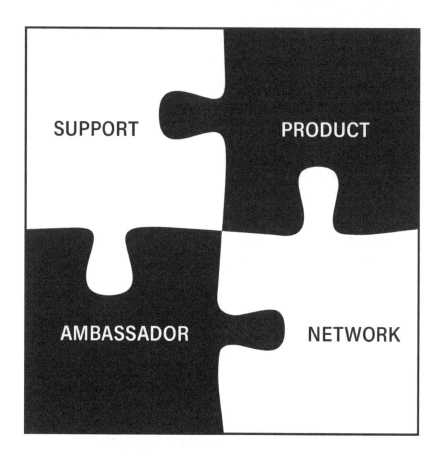

I usually share the SPAN concept with the above graphic, and it's for one crucial reason. It shows you that you don't need to worry if your community, which focuses on one of those quadrants, spills into another quadrant. It likely will. A great and thriving community probably has all four components. However, start by choosing the best fit for your first focus. Please don't get distracted in thinking you need to do them all from the start.

Also don't worry if you choose wrong. Sometimes you do. You can always change direction. One time, for example, I wanted to start a community with support. However, it became evident the focus should be on the product. Why? All the community wanted to do was talk about features and make feedback suggestions. We didn't shutter the support part. We just made it clear to the community that we heard them. We made space to help us make a better product, which was their passion.

Once we hit our goals of creating a great place for product discussions, we decided to add some areas for "networking" of partners and other users in small groups. Finally, once all the pieces were in place, support was much more successful. And this is my goal for you. When you achieve the objectives of your selected quadrant, it's time to move on to the next.

Sound good? I hope so. However, before we jump into building a structure for your community plans, I want to spend some time talking about support and product in the next couple of chapters. There are some specific experiences I've had which I think can help you along.

Chapter 8: Being On the Front Line of Community Support

Support communities will always hold a special place in my heart. Launching one from scratch is how I cut my teeth as an accidental community manager. If not for that experience, the successes, the failures, and countless long, lonely hours, you would not be reading this book.

In the previous chapter, we spoke about SPAN and how I noticed businesses were mainly creating one of those four types of communities: support, product, ambassador, or networking. In this chapter, we will go deep into support communities. In the next chapter, I'll also share advice on product communities, which I've been managing for more than five years. Read both chapters, or choose the one that is most relevant to you. By the end of these chapters, I hope my advice, experience, and specific learnings will help you hit the ground running.

There is another reason I created two specific chapters on these types of communities. I know some may think: "Aren't all communities essentially the same?" The best way I can think to showcase the difference is to say that it's like comparing a chef in high-end restaurants with a line cook in a quick-serve restaurant. It's food prep after all, right? However, just like each restaurant type is different, each community segment has its own rhythm.

This chapter and the next are really what drove me to write this book. I rarely read specific community content for running a B2B support or product community. The concept of community-building has usually been presented as a monolith. Most people who come to a support community are looking to solve a problem and reduce their frustration. Sometimes the work is not attractive, and it's hard to get colleagues to help. This is why you're reading this book. I wanted, more than anything, a reference, even for myself, to refer back to when I was knee deep and felt alone. I hope this chapter helps you explicitly, my fellow support community managers. So let's jump into it!

Why are support communities so terrifying for some? I have given this a lot of thought, and I think the most challenging part of being thrown into managing a support community is you're likely not an expert on the subject matter. Taking this on can be as terrifying as being told to take control of a plane after only playing a flight simulator game once. I mean, how exactly do you manage a community and support customers when you know little about the product? Read on. To help you, here are some ideas and strategies from my personal experience and working with others in the same boat!

Be Honest

This, to me, is the most crucial aspect. When you take over such a community, *be honest*. It's okay to say you're not an expert. However, I do recommend that you're passionate to learn more about the subject or at the very least you want to facilitate their passion. Ask them for their advice in getting started. If you have very active members in a support community, they will likely be very willing and eager to offer up their experiences, tricks, and resources. This is true if they know you're authentic about trying to learn and are open to their advice. I would recommend you also exchange with them anything you learn or cool tricks you discover. This helps build a bond and show you're one of them. Finally, keep detailed notes on your learning journey. This is last time you will have fresh eyes to help lead newer community members down a similar path.

Of course, if you are building a support community from scratch, it can be harder. You don't have those experts in the community to lean on. Don't panic, though, there is still a way forward if you lead with honesty. If you get questions in the community that you can't answer — don't hide. Be upfront about not being an expert, but also be clear that you're their advocate and you'll ensure they get an answer. And then make sure you follow through. People will appreciate your honesty, especially when you display that by advocating for them and making things happen. Eventually, you will build up your community, and with your own experiences, one day you'll be able handle the basic questions yourself. In meantime, build those alliances and help shape that crowd-sourced beacon of company knowledge everyone can benefit from.

Learn the Jargon/Shadow

When you have to take on a subject you know nothing about, it's great to build relationships and place yourself in the customer's shoes. You can do both by shadowing. When I first started working, there weren't any courses or onboarding. We learned by meeting the resident expert or person who was "voluntold" to welcome the new people. In my early career, it would be "meet Jim, he'll show you the ropes." I'm all for training and reading online, but you will understand your audience that much better when you spend time with "Jim."

Whether you are new to the company, or have been there for years, seek out these people. If the people you need can't be found at your company look at the top community contributors, who answer the majority of the questions or whom people react favourably to. Look carefully to how they express themselves. Ask them to explain the acronyms, the jargon, the most common issues people face, and create a rough idea of who to ask about what within the org.

In my experience, most people will happily talk about what they do. They love to share their knowledge. Of course, you may need to go through managers to set this time up, but it is well worth the effort, as it will inform you in ways no other experience can.

Build Your Network

Who is the go-to person for "x"? Learn their name and make friends. This is equally important internally at your company and externally in your community. There is no shame in keeping a spreadsheet or some document to remind you who to ask. Who are the leaders in the field? Connect with them online, follow their blogs and social media. Who are the customers your support or customer success team can identify as worth connecting with for knowledge sharing? Reach out and meet them. All these things can be hard at first, but I can tell you, in my case at least, it helped me be very successful and has led to lifelong friendships, even long after I moved on.

It Takes Time

Be kind to yourself. Expertise does not come overnight, but believe me, before you know it, you'll be on your way. First, you will be able to answer basic questions, and soon you'll be able to handle some of the more difficult questions. Exposure and repetition have a way of making you an expert. However, don't rush to answer questions. Continue to enable the community to answer or use your knowledge to prompt answers from the right people in your community.

You Are Not a Support Agent

If your title is community manager, you are not a support agent. Read that again. Your modus operandi is to build relationships and ensure the community members get answers to questions. You will develop the expertise to know and connect those who can help within your company and within your community. Your goal is to reduce the cost to serve by building and facilitating these relationships. It can be easy to slip into a support agent role and actually answer the questions yourself. This should be the exception and not the rule. If they've genuinely hired you as a community builder, focus on building that community, and let support handle the actual support.

When Should You Jump In?

Be clear when your company will jump into the conversation or answer the unanswered questions. Every company doing community support has some sort of SLA (service-level agreement) around this. Some keep it internal for their team; others publish an external promise for a response. What this time period is will depend on the company and the resources allocated. Some wait four hours, others 24 hours, and some even 48 hours. I know of a telecom company that focused all its support efforts on the community. In their support community, they promised customers a response to any question within 15 minutes. At the other extreme is companies that rely on their passionate fans and rarely have employees answer community questions, but it's just as swift. Think of the Apple and the Google communities, where it's almost 100 percent community-driven.

How to know what the correct time frame is? There is no perfect formula, but in this case, this is what I have used to set an internal SLA. Look at the median of your company's slowest and fastest support channels. If you offer phone support and it takes 20 minutes, and you also offer ticket or email-based support that takes about 24 hours (1,440 minutes), your community should aim for a 12-hour (730 minutes) response time. Why? The phone is immediate, so it will be generally staffed quite well. Email is one-to-one, but there can be volume issues. In a community, you have the ability of one-to-many, plus you and your team, eventually, aren't going to be answering every question. Please note, the times are merely suggestions to get started as a baseline. You have to figure out what's best for you, your team, and your own community. However, I would caution that, at a minimum, the response time should be the same as the support SLA.

The main point in creating an SLA is to encourage people to see the community as a viable option. This is why some post the SLA on their community. If you want people to take your support community seriously, you should aim to be, at the very least, faster than your current slowest channel. If people discover they gets answers quicker in your forums, they're more likely to use them. The habit will be harder to change if they know they can get things resolved faster via a ticket than coming to your community.

A small caveat: I am not suggesting that you go crazy and answer things super fast either, which could lead to superficial answers (and frustration). Community answers have a much longer shelf life and will prevent support calls. It makes sense to take the time to get it right, including adding video, PDFs, images, or anything else that enriches the answer. Also, always link to the relevant knowledge base article. If one does not exist, get it written and link to it. This helps your answer always stay accurate. I know of one company who hits the mark of 90 percent of questions answered in 90 minutes or less. It's one of the things they proudly share.

At the bare minimum for any support-focused community, I want to at least acknowledge any questions within 24 hours. When I see uncommented questions in a community, I compare it to going to a restaurant and following the sign that says "Please wait to be seated." And then no one ever comes to seat you. I know if that happens to me at a restaurant, I'll likely leave and never come back. Worse for that restaurant, I'd probably tell all my friends about the bad experience. Don't let that be the community experience you offer.

Please note, your comment on any question doesn't need to be a solution. It can be something along the lines of: "Hey, Toni! That's a great question about xxxx. I don't specifically have an answer for your situation, but here is [xxxx resource] or [xxxx resource]. Maybe a community member has had a similar experience and can suggest what they've done to solve this problem. [You could specifically mention someone with the necessary knowledge, if you're sure they are cool with jumping in to answer]. If the resources don't help, let me know, and I'll see what our team says."

Please modify the above as you need, and make sure to stay human, so it's not just a copy/paste on every question. Nothing is worse than robotic answers.

One and Done

You will likely feel the need to fight the tide of one and done — the robotic transactional nature of support communities. I won't hide that most support spaces are notorious for people coming to scratch the itch and never return. Every support community has to battle this. The truth is, if people find their answers, even if they don't sign up, it's still a success. I know this can be hard to accept. Rather than focus on the negative, focus on the opportunity to make the community something more. Encourage people in your workflows and touchpoints to share how they use a product or service to do more. Give them examples of content and questions/opportunities to connect. People using business tools, especially if they are a team of one, will value a sense of belonging. However, never overdo it or be annoying by requesting more from those who prefer the transactional nature of your community. It's just a fact that most interactions in a support community will be transient. That doesn't mean you can't seek out and nurture a core of passionate people within your community. I just want to caution you against this feeling that your members *have* to be doing more.

Time is an Enemy

You have a problem, and you do a search in Google. You land on a forum thread where the question asker has a similar situation. However, you notice it's from 2012, and the answer is outdated. Foiled again! How do you handle that? Add to your tasks (or your mod team) to regularly look at old conversations and update the answers. You can point old posts to more recent discussions as well.

One company I know has the policy to ensure all answers are linked to the relevant knowledge base (KB) article, and if one is not created, to ensure one is. Think of it as "community knowledge-centred support." This way, the community answer always points to the so-called "one source of truth," no matter how long ago it was answered. To me, this is the best-in-class solution of very well-organized and mature support and community organization. Don't we all want to strive to be the best in class? While it might be hard, try to consider how your community answers will age. What is your process to handle that?

One company's answer to this problem is to create categories around every version number. When a new version is released, they create a new category. They also have a category for more universal software questions. This helps in a couple of ways:

- They can close/archive older versions of discussions to avoid frustration, so they're not the first result that shows in search — or it's clear they're out of date.
- They can add a message at the top of the category to point visitors to the latest version.
- Take quick action if prior solutions do not work for the current version and update their community.

Some companies don't use categories; they use tags. This way they can have an answer for multiple versions, searchable via one master tag. As you can see, there are several ways to tackle the time problem. Spend the time to map out your strategy as early as you can. Don't ignore this problem, as you will have to deal with old answers or software versions at some point.

I hope you found this chapter helpful, although I am sure there is some advice I have simply forgotten. Nonetheless, I hope I was able to get you started on your support community journey. In the next chapter, I'll share my specific learnings and advice for those building a *product* community. Surprisingly, there are many commonalities between the two, which might be why I love them both so much. Onwards!

Chapter 9: Your Product Sucks!

In the previous chapter, we talked about support communities. They hold a special place in my heart, but so do product communities. Before being paid to do web marketing, I was a product manager, and all my time was spent obsessing on products, reviews, and online reputation (among other things).

Where support communities are usually about customers solving their problems or sharing frustrations, product communities are mostly about customer learning, sharing, and complaining (ahem, suggesting) how to make the product or service better. Anyone who has managed or been part of a product community will tell you there will be countless threads along these lines: "Why does your brand not have XYZ features that would make my job/life so much easier?" Another concern is an inundation of "suggestions" from your customer base that may overwhelm the team. Of course, there is also the fear of a rant about why your product/company sucks gaining traction in your community.

That fear is usually the biggest to overcome when trying to make a community program happen in the most conservative companies. I understand why. They worry about being on stage, and all eyes are trained on them. It can be tempting to silence (i.e., delete or ignore) the negative and just praise your fans. The reality is that if you have a space for people, such as your customers, to talk, someone will make a comment, and maybe one you're not comfortable with.

Before you or your company decides to run for the hills, I would like to argue that the community is actually where you *want* negative conversations to happen. I would rather have this discussion in a space where, presumably, I have the email of the poster and, potentially, their customer history. You have so much more context and information to work with than a random/anonymous account on a social network writing negative comments. It could even be a competitor just out there causing trouble.

This can happen. I've seen it firsthand. Many years ago, we started to see a few really surprisingly negative reviews about Vanilla on a software review site. One day, the site changed how reviewers were identified. In this case, it now showed the LinkedIn profile of the reviewers. Low and behold, a couple of staff at a competitor had given us 1-star reviews. Suffice to say, those were removed when we contacted the review company. I learned that some people can't compete based on their own product. They need to tear down others for fear of their own inferiority. It still sucked for that whole time, seeing those 1-star ratings. We knew we had a good product, but there was no way to handle it but comment on the reviews offering to talk about their experiences.

This is why I say, don't fear the community. Make it *the* space where people can leave (hopefully respectful) criticism because you will also be able to address it and turn it into a chance to demonstrate *great* customer service. However, and this is important, you should address negative comments with as much transparency you can, in a tone that does not sound like a PR assistant wrote it for you. Community is about intimacy and the people. Try not to trot out the BS in this space. Your goal is to build trust. People wanting to buy your product are looking at how you handle things.

A word of caution, though, if your company *does* suck — they might want to work on fixing that, and, if not, you should consider working at a new company.

Community is the least of their problems. However, if your company has a good product and has built a strong community, your community members will usually swarm on the negative.

In my experience, companies worried about a barrage of criticism usually are those that don't listen to their customers. Their customers have legitimate reasons to be upset. On the positive, if the company has issues, creating a space for customer voices is something you can point to as a positive — especially if they are engaged in an honest way. This tells your community you are trying to do better and connect. It takes courage, but it will garner respect.

Overall, a community will provide a net positive by offering a great space to get feedback on your product and really get close to your customers in a way your product teams will find invaluable. Nonetheless, if you are new to the game, it can be daunting to take this on. As I did in the previous chapter, here is a non-exhaustive list of advice for product communities:

Handling the Negative

This, to me, has always been the most challenging skill. I won't lie. When I work for a company, I generally am there because I have a passion for their product, so the negative hurts hard. Anyone who has spent time building anything knows how much it sucks to have people only point out flaws and never appreciate the beauty. However, we have to face it. Some people live to watch the world burn. They may wear the most fantastic leather shoes in the world, but all they shout about is that one time a pebble snuck into their shoe. Although it took them a second to remove the pebble, and it never happened again, it's all they can focus on. These people do exist. I hope you never have them in the community (or in your life), but unlike in life, where you can avoid them, you can't in the community. So, let's accept that this can happen. But how can we, as community builders, deal with it?

The most important thing is not to take it personally. I would make sure you have clear guidelines that ask people to discuss the product or ideas while not attacking the person or company. We have to start from a place of assuming everyone (in the community) is collectively here to connect and to move the company/product/service forward for the better. There is nothing wrong with having rules about tone.

Also, if the comment is well-worded but tough to take, resist the action to delete it. It's about trust and authenticity. No company is perfect. Customers researching your company want to know the "dirty secrets" or the negative. But they are also looking carefully at how *you* (as you represent the company) respond to them. People will notice if you are rude, or delete or close comments without answering.

This is why you need a plan. As part of your situational playbook (which we will go into greater detail about in chapter 20) should cover handling negative reviews. This may include how to grade the severity of the review (e.g., is this something needing immediate action?), who needs to be notified, how a response will be given, who to escalate to, what the response time SLA is, and other company-specific actions. It can be based on, or mirror how, your company would react to a social media post. The only difference being you may have direct access to the customer's email address and purchase history to know the validity of any claim. It should also have clear guidance on tone and next steps. Yes, it may also require you to involve other teams, who may respond in the community, but it should all be laid out so there are no surprises.

You should also have a process, or be ready to handle, "pile-ons." As I mentioned earlier, the situational playbook would cover most of the challenging aspects of running a community. What is the plan if other users begin to pile on into this negative thread? What is your process?

For example, in a Vanilla-powered community, you may use the "sink" feature, which avoids bumping the discussion up as new comments are made. This gives you time to respond — and prevent a pile-on — to a highly negative review. You lay out the criteria for using "sink" in your situational playbook and outline who needs to be consulted in crafting a response depending on the severity.

My parting thought for you on the negative reviews is that it *will* happen, but you can control how you react to them. Transparency, honesty, and promptness in responding are the best way to show your community you care. In really healthy communities, where you lead by this example, you'll be surprised at how the community may intercede on your behalf and come to your defence. This is something I have seen many times. A community reaction to negativity directly impacts how they feel the company treats the legitimate concerns. Your current and potential customers are watching you. Act accordingly for their benefit, if not for the original poster.

Product Team Involvement

You cannot have a product-focused community without product team involvement. There, I have said it for you. Show it to your boss if they disagree. You *need* the product team involved. They don't necessarily need to be present and posting in the community (which is so cool and always the dream), but their support is crucial to your success. You likely don't have the insights or the ability to make a change, and may not even have product experience.

Here's the truth, though: a product team loves to have feedback from "real" users or customers — as long as it's realistic and detailed. So, your product team will likely lurk in your spaces anyway. Depending on volume, I encourage you to create weekly (or monthly) meetings to surface community sentiment, user stories, frustrations, and ideas with the product team.

Part of getting the product team involved is giving your community insight and access. This is a crucial aspect of the product community. If people are passionate about your brand, making your community *the* place to get the latest news and official "leaks," makes your community sticky. It's a more natural space for people to geek out with the community about the things you are building than in a vast ocean of social.

The most crucial thing in getting product teams involved is making the community content part of their workflow and not imposing yours on them. Do they use Jira? Productboard? If so, make the ideas go into those tools via API, Webhook, or other community integrations. It's relatively painless to do, and while it may require some dev work, it is crucial in larger organizations. Having your customers' idea and improvements show up in their tools ensures they see and can action these ideas. We don't need to get hung up on where it happens. If your community is being heard, you all win!

Feedback Loops

If you ask people to vote on ideas or discuss features, you need a feedback loop. Don't be a company that asks for feedback and never gives any information back. If you do, you're being a real "askhole." If any part of your community has a space where the expectation is that people will share their concepts, vote on ideas or share feedback, make sure someone from your company — and it doesn't need to be you (but it may be) — gives feedback from the company POV. In your role, it can be as simple as acknowledging the idea. Ideally, though, you have built relationships with the product team, where you can have them give the feedback, or they can give you guidance on ideas. "Great idea! Tell us more about your user story" or "Great minds think alike. It's on the roadmap for Q4 — more details forthcoming." Simple phrases can go so far in making your community feel heard. Ignore their feedback at the peril that it will stop. No one wants to talk to a wall. Don't make them feel they are doing your market research without appreciation.

Too Much Feedback

Sometimes there is a scenario where people have the following concern: "Sure, we want to ask our community for their ideas, but we will get too much feedback to handle. We did this before, and it just led to frustrations. The PMs were stressed due to the volume of ideas, and the community was upset that we did not respond with feedback." These are very legitimate concerns for a large organization. It's one thing to have a community of 400 to 500 people and a different thing to have one with millions of members. So how do you handle it?

I call it "roadmap-focused feedback." In a private customer area, you list the priorities your team is working on, and in specific threads, ask for targeted feedback and suggestions around this list. You can make it a program with weekly, monthly, or quarterly threads on specific topics. This keeps it focused and makes it easier for your product team to engage. So even if you get numerous ideas will be highly relevant to the tasks the product team is already working on. You will also be able to see which ideas resonate most with your audience, either by allowing them to vote or by merging similar ideas.

Another way to handle feedback is a monthly digest. This comes from my friend Nichole Devolites. In one of her community roles, she would collect the feedback once a month, putting into a digest and summarizing it for the product team. Once done, she would schedule a discussion with the team. At the end of that meeting, someone would be appointed to respond within a set timeframe. The most important fact, of course, is always communication with the community. To ensure this, Nichole would add a clear message to top of the feedback group. What did it include? Clear language about the entire process, so users knew what to expect and also an expected response time after submitting such feedback. If they found one item had overwhelming feedback or was similar, she'd put out one discussion post on that specific subject. In the body of the post, she would mention all those that provided feedback on that topic, so they would be aware of the company response.

Focus Groups and Calls

Not all community-building happens on the forum. I know this may be shocking for some to hear from me. As a matter of fact, I implore you to consider supplementing your online community with other ways for people to connect. It doesn't all have to happen in the text format on the forum. These moments can be curated, more intimate, and immediate.

Consider secret community groups for beta testers, where they get an early sneak peek watch party of a product release. I am a big fan of these kinds of group calls. I know many have Zoom overload, but it's still a solid way to meet and connect with others in the community who cannot travel.

I've held weekly, biweekly, and monthly calls with community members when running a product community, and it's always been so insightful. The product/marketing people are always eager to join and talk with real users. What do they think? How can they do better? What are the things they would like to see? My job is to be a master connector to make it happen — or at the very least, pass along the feedback constructively. When done well, you will get positive reactions from the product team and community.

A quick note on the size of the audience on calls. This is not a call with 300 people. I try to keep it to less than eight people outside the company, with myself as host. Why nine? Is it science? Not really. It's just that nine people are the number of people who can fit on one Zoom screen comfortably. It's okay if you have 10 or 12 people. I am merely suggesting you may get overwhelmed by 15 or 20 voices. This way, everyone has time to add their input. Also, by limiting the seats, you make sure you choose the best people to be there — and by the best, I mean the most thoughtful, willing to share, diverse backgrounds, and use cases.

Finally, I like to make it very clear that call wills not be recorded — so people can speak openly — and that "camera on" is optional. I try to replicate the intimacy of in-person connection as much as possible. And by not recording, you make sure people come, instead of just waiting for the recording later.

Nurturing and Finding Your Fans

This is the best and most exciting part of the community-building, at least for me. In a product community, this is where you can identify your fans. They can become your community superstars. Identifying people early is much like scouting in baseball. The community member comes out of nowhere and is pure raw joy and excitement. Your role is to identify and coach them into something more.

There are many methods to identify people. It usually starts when they are doing something most people don't do: volunteering to answer someone else's question, with the correct info, in a tone of voice that is empathic and helpful. They show proper knowledge of how the product works and explain things in a concise way. People also generally react positively to their contributions, because they add value to the conversations at hand and the community overall.

You should consider how to handle these people. It could be a commitment curve, or some way to track people with tasks, until they get into a leadership role. It can start with a simple personal message of thanks and evolve into greater responsibility over time with mini-projects. Of course, these are independent people, who can do as they please, but some of my deepest online friendships are with people I met who shared a similar passion.

Let's also add a word of caution: don't rely on one person too much in your community. This can make your helpful member burn out due to being overwhelmed.

For Your Friends in Marketing

Next up, I want to call out our friends in marketing, and likely, either the place you came from or the department you report into. The product community is a great source of wonderful case studies, recommendations, and reviews. You should be protecting your community from being too much of a marketing space, but the content of a product community is inherently a marketer's dream.

To that end, it's an awful idea to let your marketing teams post their marketing content without a personal voice, or include any content that lacks consideration about "what's in it for the community." Community is about connection and two-way sharing. It's not about yelling at people and hoping they listen or click to download the latest piece of content.

You can positively impact how marketing interacts with the community and ensure your community benefits. Marketing in most companies has a budget for swag and can be your biggest cheerleader. Including the community in marketing, like holding a video contest to show off how they use the product, with a nice prize, could be something fun for the community and satisfy marketing needs at the same time.

A community can be a great place to test ideas on the packaging, the approach, and the tone in your marketing. People who are passionate and feel like they have a stake in the product will love to be involved. Identifying them might include asking in your annual community survey and matching it up to their community behaviour.

You Are Not a Product (Marketer)

Just as I needed to remind those of my friends in support communities that they aren't support agents, I want to remind those working in a product community, you are not a marketer. Your outward focus is not about pushing product, lead capture, or MQLs (marketing qualified leads). Your job is relationship building, connecting, collaborating, and empowering the members of your community. The by-product of your activities will enrich your product marketing teams.

This is an important distinction I need to make, even for myself, as a former product marketer. At first, it was hard to separate myself from the marketing first mindset. The word "community" in your title should be primary. This does not mean you need to ignore your experience. I am merely suggesting you approach your community with the right POV. Whatever your internal KPI is, it doesn't matter outwardly. Your tone and conduct in the community are that of a champion. You need to think about the inherent value of asks and offers from your company towards your membership. Your success relies on the trust they have for you. Yes, it requires a mind shift, but you got this. I just want to make sure you are clear to yourself and your team — your role is thinking about community first and marketing secondary.

One final thought on KPIs. You still need to have a business impact, and you should strive for that. However, do your best to think about the community members first and the value tied to achieving the KPI. If the KPI is driving leads, think about the kinds of things that the community, or potential community, people will find valuable enough to make them share their contact details. This is how you work towards a win for both parties.

If you're going to be running a product community, I am so excited for you! You have a chance to have a significant impact on your organization. Some of the most excellent and respected brands have seen success by creating a solid community around their brand. You have the chance to be the person who helps your company do the same. You have a unique role in bringing fans' passions to the community around a product and facilitating their voices within your company. Your role is essential, and the amount of value you can bring to your organization is a game-changer. A company with a robust and vibrant community is a powerful and hard-to-beat competitor. I hope the above advice helps get you on your way!

Chapter 10: Don't Ship Your Community Without CARGO!

By now you should have gathered all this sweet, sweet info from your team and customers during your investigations. Up next is the fun, empowering, and best part. It's time to consider your community plan.

When you're done this chapter, you will have the recipe to build a one-page document tying in all the information from your discovery and what kind of community you will be building. Your MVP discussions should also guide you as you create this plan. As a quick recap on MVP — you should have this information: What do the people coming to your community want and what do the most valuable people internally (the stakeholders) care about that your community can impact?

At this point, you should also have your SPAN selected, and hopefully, you have some ideas on the metrics, goals, and outcomes to consider for your community. These ideas are not yet carved in stone — things do change — but our goal now is to organize all your findings into something useful. This is why I created the CARGO framework.

The idea of CARGO came to me one fine day after working on hundreds of communities. I realized the most successful communities addressed five key elements, and I wanted to create an easy, repeatable way for other community builders to find that same success. It's easy to get bogged down in a community plan and write out an essay. No one ends up reading it, and it's too complex for your executive team to understand. Make a detailed document for yourself, but use CARGO as your guiding light. In fact, I *encourage* you to write out a more detailed plan, with clear actions and steps to achieve your goals. However, at this point, our objective is to stay focused, clear, and brief. Communities need to be built on clear solid foundations!

Are you ready to get going? I know I am! Find a piece of paper, or open a new document on your computer, and let's build your CARGO plan! It all begins with the first letter:

Concept

What is the concept or subject the community is about? Too many times, a community concept is too much "on the nose." For example, should a company like Procter & Gamble create an online community for customers using their Crest toothpaste, or would it be better for them to create an online community for those wishing to discuss dental health? Should a company that makes plumbing equipment create a community for support of their products, or would it be better to create a space where plumbers can share tactics, images, projects, and get advice?

Spend some time on the concept, and not in a vacuum of the boardroom. Ask the audience you have identified in your discovery steps. What projects are they working on? How can you help them be more successful at their work? With their boss? What resources do they wish existed? How can you help them elevate their skills? Be better at their job? Make connections? Stay educated? Give back?

Don't get hung up on writing the concept with them at this point. Talk with your audience to understand their pains, dreams, and motivations. This is also the time to balance things with your internal goals. Which parts of your audience does your company care about...and which do they not? You do not need to create a space for everyone. Or maybe you only create it for a portion of your potential membership and open it up further in the future. Stick with the groups most likely to have an impact and enthusiastically participate.

The end result of all this talking is to inform what you can create that could help satisfy both internal and external MVPs. Before any decision is made, consider whether you have support from your company, external stakeholders, or an enthusiastic group. There is no point, for example, creating a community where plumbing novices ask questions, if you have no one with plumbing experience answering them (at least to start). Don't hope these people will "show up."

Key Questions
- Why does this community exist?
- Who is/isn't my target audience?
- Will people find this space helpful to solve their personal goals?
- Will my management/additional resources support such a concept?
- Does my concept align with goals/outcomes expected by key stakeholders?

Acquisition

What's a party without guests? For a community to be successful, we need people to actually take part. This is a key concept in igniting the passion and fire of people who are going to partake in this beautiful concept you've created. We now need people to participate.

This starts with the idea that we need to make sure it's recognized, organizational-wide, that this space exists. Or in other words, how is the visibility of your community?

If it's a support community, will people see this as an option to get support on the help page? Can people find the link to your community easily on your website? There is a simple step you can check too. If your company communications make it easier to find your Facebook or Twitter accounts than it is to find your community, you have an issue to fix. Include your community information it in an audio message when people call your company. Drop an invitation inside the box your product comes in. Make sure your community content is in the marketing newsletters.

Visibility is only half the battle. The other part of this includes them dipping in to create an account. For that to happen, we need to consider things like: What value are we offering? How will we get people to care about joining? What are the emotional triggers we hope to evoke? What do we want people to feel/experience when they enter our community? This is the not-so-easy part, but the interviews during your concept stage should help put you on the path to solving the kinds of problems and pains people have. You may have created a small test group on Slack or Facebook to prove the concept, but now it's time to use these experiences to consider what things this audience cares about that will prompt them to be part of your community.

One idea I've always liked is how Richard Millington has identified specific emotional pairs in community-building. It's a solid idea to tie them to how you acquire your audience.

Richard has noted three big emotions to consider with community-building: excitement, fear, and frustration. They will manifest themselves as inspiration, validation, and resolution. So Richard recommends, that you aim to create communities around these three things:

- Excitement and Inspiration: Focuses on best ideas, advice, encouraging repeat visits. Content is around best-of lists or best advice.
- Fear and Validation: Works by playing on fear and the validation people can get from the community, where they can see how they are doing compared to others, and also get validation for their choices. This is handy, especially for people potentially working alone, and thus, the community becomes their go-to space to not feel so isolated. The content includes reviews, experience using various tools, working-out-loud threads, seeking advice from others.
- Frustration and Resolution: Most support communities focus on what happens when "x" is not working and then helping people resolve the issue. The content features top solutions, video how-to, FAQs.

Make these emotional triggers clear in your acquisition messaging.

Key Questions
- How easy is it to find the community?
- How do we tell our customers the community exists, or how will be discovered?
- What is the value proposition we are offering to get them in the door?
- What emotional experiences do we want to appeal to them?

Retention

What will keep them coming back? This builds on the aspect of acquisition, in terms of creating the content and value that matters. You want to become known as "the space" to be on in terms of your topic or concept.

You acquired people by using those emotions we identified earlier. Now we can add the elements of segmentation. What will be of interest to each cohort of your audience? What will experts care about? What will new people care about? Most importantly, how will you talk to these segments regularly? What kinds of content programming can you create? What are the regular touchpoints? What internal company resources and tools will you need? In essence, what are the things you can do to keep the community top of mind, so they come back? For example, ensure your monthly release notes get posted first and exclusively to the community. This allows those in the community immediate access and ability to comment/ask questions first. Another idea: A monthly spotlight in the community, with a creator AMA on something they built with your product and how they did it. And another idea: Weekly behind-the-scenes tips from your engineering team, where you facilitate a conversation about why they did what they did? It's a combination of content marketing and interactivity with the audience. You can use your blog or KB articles as sources of inspiration.

However, I should add a word of caution. You do not need to lay out your whole content program in your CARGO sheet. What you need to mark down is a commitment to regular programming and which people and departments are to be leveraged. We will go into content planning in another chapter. What should be listed in your CARGO plan are the commitments to create regular programming —

daily, weekly, monthly, or quarterly — using help from product, engineering, marketing, or success teams.

It's also not only about content programs — it's also about the process. For example, what triggers can be created? Maybe you consider using marketing automation to email community members a monthly digest based on "can't miss content." It could be your customer success managers (CSMs), if your company has such roles, regularly reminding customers that the community is an extra resource to find inspiration. Another simple thing could be support teams adding a link to the community in their signatures. Any touchpoint that can be a reminder can help in building those habits.

Key Questions
- How will you get people to return to the community?
- Why should people care to return?
- What reminders/touches can you plan?
- Which departments/technology can assist?

Goals

What is the goal of your community? As far as I am concerned, everything up to now was just an appetizer. This is the most crucial aspect of the framework. With concrete goals and tying them to numeric results, you, as the community builder, give yourself ammunition for your worth and investment in your programs.

So how do you start? Begin with the main business goals that matter to the internal MVPs — especially those stakeholders that control the money and your career destiny. Have a conversation. You can also do some deep discovery with other department members for advice before you approach the lead stakeholder. Shadow a marketing manager and ask them what matters to them before you hit up the VP of Marketing, so you're ready to talk their language and understand their pains.

You will want to also have (if you haven't already) conversations with the community you hope to attract. What are the things people in the community care about? How do we translate the stakeholder concerns into things the external MVPs care about? For example, your internal MVP might be the VP of Product. They want actionable product ideas from the community based on the roadmap objectives. What does this mean for you? It means creating a space for the community to suggest ideas and vote on other members' ideas. It is crucial that you tie some numbers to that goal to see success. For example, you could agree that 10 accepted product ideas per quarter means you are on track. You don't need a laundry list of goals, but they should be impactful, and there should be one per leader. Be laser-focused on that goal.

I want to be clear: this does not mean you don't, or can't, measure community health metrics or sense of community. These are important for your job. For example, you can measure community satisfaction or whether you have an active and engaged audience consuming content. However, as harsh as it sounds to some of you, this does not matter for most stakeholders. By nature, people are selfish, and want their area of interest to succeed. Share with stakeholders only the numbers and data that will impact *their* objectives. You can certainly share other data, but I prefer to keep conversations focused. Our goal is to make them look good and help their cause. The more you can do that, the more you increase the likelihood you will get their buy-in for your programs.

While we want people to enjoy the community, sadly, if it doesn't translate into success for business goals, you eventually put yourself into the dreaded "talk." The conversation about "what business value does community bring?" or "what value are you bringing?" should not be something you scramble to figure out after the question is asked. It should be something intentional, which you have a conversation about as early as possible in your community-building.

Here are some ideas for community goals to consider:

- How is the community translating to customer satisfaction with a brand?
- How many upsells/cross-sells/upgrades came from active community members?
- How many new prospects is your community converting?
- How many tickets do community members create vs. non-members?
- How many reviews, case studies, or advocate activities are generated?

You can take an existing business and overlay it against your community data. Don't let your community data live in a silo. How are community members scoring your Net Promoter Score ®
 (NPS®) vs. other customers? Get the data and show the impact.

The answers to these questions are what piques stakeholder interest. Also, don't fear how or where to get data. Most companies have a data person, who is more than eager to help answer these questions. If not, your stakeholder will likely also be willing to help, because, as we mentioned before, you are helping their cause.

Some will argue the merits of focusing on your stakeholders instead of the community audience, but I want nothing but success for you. You should do your best to hit stakeholder goals and then translate it into value for the community. Leading and focusing on the numeric impact, especially in the B2B world, is how you prove your value and get the resources you need long term.

Key Questions
- What are the main goals that matter to each *stakeholder*?
- How can we translate this to *the community*?
- Are they SMART goals — Specific, Measurable, Achievable, Relevant, and Timely?

Outcomes

We are in the home stretch. What specific overarching, time-bound outcomes can define success? This is where you want to visualize what success will look like for your community long term. Need inspiration? Ask your internal MVPs what would make them happy for your community at the end of the year.

We want to set a strong outcome with numbers that can be measured. This will be your anchor outcome, which you can measure, modify, or tweak as the year progresses. However, this is not an anchor to drown yourself with. If your community does not have the outcomes that create impact, have an honest discussion about modifying what you can deliver. Also, you should be sharing results regularly with your internal MVPs, so you have time for these discussions to course correct. Don't wait a year! Have regular meetings on your community progress with these stakeholders at least once a quarter. It's important to ensure that your community is at the heart of the company's goals and not something they can do without.

As I am fond of saying when I talk about outcomes, consider if you coached an NHL hockey team. Your goal as a general manager is to make the NHL playoffs, but the ultimate outcome is to win the Stanley Cup. If your season starts off poorly, with too many losses, you may consider a trade or bringing someone up from the minors. You try to shake things up. The longer the season goes on, the closer and more accurately you can see how you are achieving your outcome. The outcome is winning the Stanley Cup — your North Star.

Some examples of outcomes:

- 20 percent of product ideas implemented coming from the community in a calendar year
- 15 percent annual reduction of tickets
- 75 percent service subscription renewal rate by community members at years' end
- 30 percent of community members answering questions instead of staff per year
- 40 knowledge base articles written by the community per year

Key Questions

- When the year comes to an end, what is your overarching vision for the community?
- What are the specific and measurable things that will define this success?

Let's now put this all together. The following is a CARGO plan I put together for the FAKE company — a company making software for designers to manipulate photos and video. This is just to give you an idea of what it should look like.

Concept

We are a software company making tools for designers in the B2B space. Our tool is not used by retail customers. The community will be focused on encouraging peer-to-peer support on ramping up customers.

Acquisition

Start with inviting designers who previously used our retail product with non-free email addresses. We will also work closely with other parts of the organization to identify potential founding members from our CRM. Aim for Q1 of this year to have a solid group of 100 founding members. We will work with our marketing team on messaging that makes them feel special, want to share their expertise, and be inspired by others. Ensure our website and marketing materials clarify how to join the community by the end of Q2 this year.

Retention

By creating a go-to space, we feel we will become *the* place for users of our new Pro-software. Our goal is to ensure there is daily content for inspiration, so we will include tutorials and host AMAs on how the results were achieved. We will also offer unique content, and reward contributors who make amazing content, with access to the company product and our team, exclusive deals, and more. We plan to create an industry-leading newsletter from the content to help attract more people.

Goals

Support deflection is essential for our head of support. Have the community become a source of self-support by elevating our external MVPs and having them answer the majority of questions. We will encourage this by recognizing the question answers, with points, badges, and perks for the most answers given. They will also get free licenses to the products and upgrades, as long as they stay active by logging in 50% of the time within any month and answering at least three questions. We plan to introduce the program 30–60 days after the community launch. Members should answer about 50% of questions by the end of Q3.

Our product team wants product suggestions and to find the features that will make the product stickier. Major focus on what incumbents do that we can do better. We'll create a space for our best customers to share product ideas. The goal is to turn over a minimum of five ideas a quarter to the product team for improvements.

Outcomes

Our main successful outcome is to see that the community answers 75 percent of questions without our own team needing to jump in by the end of Q2 of next year.

For our product team, we expect, by Q4, to start a monthly report on new ideas. Aiming for one to two accepted product changes a quarter starting by Q1 of next year.

I hope this example helps get you in the right frame of mind and gets your creative juices flowing!

Now one more thing before we move on, I want to ensure you get maximum impact with your CARGO plan. I want you to focus on the investment. One is the investment in your skills. I appreciate you reading this book, but don't stop. See if you can get your manager's support to continue your learning journey by allocating budget and time to take courses. At the very least, I encourage you to read business blogs or subscribe to newsletters in the community, marketing, customer success, and customer experience spaces.

The second investment is in making sure your company is *invested* in the community. This means making your company, beyond your team, care about this community. This includes having regular conversations, reporting up, sharing successes. Silence is deadly for you as a community manager. You need to speak up and share. You need to lead. Be a silo breaker. Make sure you involve other team members as you build your plan — their buy-in is essential.

If you follow the outline of CARGO, I know you will be successful. I have seen it help so many, but don't worry if you can't finish your CARGO plan now. You can change it as you need. And besides, you should revisit it regularly to keep yourself on the right path. It's your document, to ensure you are doing the right things to meet your goals. I promise, by the end of the book, you'll be more than ready to ship your community.

Chapter 11: SaaSy Goals

We've talked about goals and outcomes in the previous chapter, but I wanted to specifically talk to my software as a service (SaaS) community friends. If you are building a B2B community at this point in history, it's quite likely you're in the SaaS space. That's just how things are now. But once you are in the SaaS industry for any length of time, you quickly learn there are three main goals at the top of mind for the executive team:

- Increase bookings and revenue
- Net revenue retention
- Reduce cost to serve

I've had many conversations with senior leaders in this space, and their goals always end up in one of these buckets. However, especially if you are new, aligning your community to these three outcomes can be daunting. I wanted to provide you something a bit more tactical if you found yourself in this situation.

Increase Bookings and Revenue

This is likely the most common goal you will have. It's about leads or, in SaaS, subscriptions — pure and simple. Another way you may hear it is MQLs/SQLs (Marketing/Sales Qualified Leads). At advanced companies with keen marketing programs, they worry about Sales Ready Leads (SRL) — the folks showing the behaviours where they are most likely to buy. So how do you go about increasing those numbers? Of course, you can't boldly go into a community and say, "Hey, we need y'all to fill in some forms." That's not how it works.

The main thing you can control is content. What I mean by that is facilitating content creation for marketing teams and making sure your best and brightest have a space to write amazing content. We've covered content earlier in the book, so you know how important content is for SEO and creating shareable content. If you community is public-facing (no login required), there are tons of opportunities for ranking and sharing.

If a public community is not possible, your focus might be less about new sales and more about cross-sells and upsells. This is because the customers already have access to the community. In this case, there are three things you aim to achieve in the community:

1. Showcase the value of what they bought via great content (more on that in the next section)
2. Make them aware of potential cross-sells
3. Make them aware of possible upsells

This means showcasing to your current community of customers the product they have and what more they could do by purchasing other products or upgrades. How does one do this? By inviting customers already using the product to share their experiences and have them create content showcasing how they use it.

Now some of you have the first part down, but you may be asking, how do I measure any of this? This is the essential point of this chapter. We live in a digital world, and your company has many touchpoints. You want to ensure your community is part of that tracking. Suppose your company has a marketing automation tool, like HubSpot or Marketo, or a CRM, like Salesforce. In that case, you want to make sure your tool captures customer community activity, so you can show the influence on deals.

For example:
- Who are the prospects who found your company via the community?

- Who are the prospects who bought/upgraded because of the community?
- What was the content read/consumed from the community to help a deal?

This is not an exhaustive list, but you should be asking these questions and, hopefully, getting access to this data to prove your value.

Even if you are not using huge or expensive tools, or have little access, most analytics tools have attribute reports, where you can see where your community had an impact in deals. You can confidently account for a percentage of buyers who had community as part of their purchase journey.

The data analysts in your company will be happy to help you if you direct them with the above requests. We all know your community has an impact. Now you need to make sure you measure it and show it!

Net Revenue Retention (NRR)

Net revenue retention (NRR) is a buzzy term related essentially to keeping your customers happy and not churning (i.e., cancelling). So, to be a bit more technical, NRR is shown as the percentage of recurring revenue retained from existing customers, including expansion revenue, downgrades, and cancels. The closer to 100% or above, the better.

To simplify it further for you, it's truly a measure of two things — perceived value and happiness with outcomes. If your members are happy and feel the product/service is valuable, they are less likely to churn. This means they are more loyal. The more loyal and satisfied they are, the more likely they are to advocate on your behalf — or in the simplest terms, recommend you.

The goal of the community builder does not change. It's to create a great space, connect community people together, and make sure they see value as quickly as possible. This can be from content programming to events to networking and everything we covered earlier.

I want to focus on what to measure to showcase you're doing a great job. What you want to measure is advocacy activity. How many case studies are you able to gather from community members? How many G2 crowd reviews can you connect? How are people scoring you on a customer effort score (CES) or NPS® (Net Promoter Score ®) survey?

The main thing to know about any scores in this instance is the following: the better the scorers the more likely those folks will be to recommend your business and, also less likely to churn. Also, if your community is a source of these higher scores, the more you can make the case you are helping reduce churn.

How to get tactical with measuring this? Work with your customer success organization or whoever runs the overall NPS® for your company. Overlay your customer activity in the community and your company data. The goal will be to show that the more active people are in the community, the more likely they will recommend your brand. All the times I have seen this done, the community usually comes out ahead. If not, you, hopefully, get some guidance from customer comments on what you can do better.

If your organization is not doing NPS® measurement, you can also would check out CES measurement –- which just checks how hard or easy people need to work to find answers. Whatever you choose, you should regularly be thinking of a way to show the value of what you build. If a community is helping reduce the effort of your customers, it's a bright light in keeping them using your product — and you need to tell that story!

Reduce Cost to Serve

This is the classic around support communities, and it's about reducing customer frustration when it comes to using your product. However, from the executive standpoint, it's about lowering support costs by ticket deflection or the ever-more-direct idea of customer avoidance. The goal is that the community acts as level 1 support to solve the most common questions, so your support team can focus on the more complex issues.

Essentially, the human-to-human support is a very costly channel. Community support is, by far, a much more cost-effective solution. It allows companies to scale support without them significantly increasing head count.

As before, I am not going into how to *create* a support community — it's way beyond the scope of this chapter — and you can check out Chapter 8 if you need a refresh. I want to focus on how to measure and share what you do in the community, so you look like the community-building rock star you are.

There are a couple of ways deflection can be looked at. One is the idea of the "self-service ratio," where you take how many total active users you have in your community and divide by the total number of users submitting a ticket.

So, for example, if you had 1,000 members in your community and 100 tickets, the ratio would be 10:1. In other words, for every 10 members active in the community, only one submitted a ticket. You can measure this over time as a benchmark and show how the ratio improves.

However, we want to get you a step further — and more numeric. We want you to be able to tell your management about the savings, because we all know money talks. Here is the breakdown to get there:

1. Find out the cost of a call or a ticket — non-community contact. Your support leader should know it.
2. What are the number of sessions created by people coming to your community? Use Google Analytics or something similar to measure.
3. Create an exit survey. You could use Qualtrics, Hotjar, Alchemer. It should have at least these three questions:
   1. Did you come to the community today to find a solution to an issue you were having?
   2. If yes, did you find information on the community that led you to a solution?
   3. If yes, did your visit avoid the necessity to contact our team?
4. This will give you the percentage of people who found a solution and did not need to take another step. This will leave you with the number of sessions deflected.
5. Multiply the number of sessions deflected by the cost of calling support.

So, as an example: A call to your non-community support is $50. In a month, there are 5,000 sessions to your community. Your survey results show that 10 percent of people found the answer without contacting support. Therefore, you had 500 sessions that got their answer on the community at $50 a pop. This means that this month you "saved" your company $25,000.

Formula in action:

- 5,000 sessions to your community in a month
- 10 percent of respondents reported deflection

- 500 deflected sessions @ $50 (ticket cost)
- "Saved": $25,000

The savings are not 100 percent, though, as there is a cost to your community. So, you will want to take this number and subtract your community budget cost (tools + people) and then divide by budget to get to your ROI.

"Support Savings" – Community Budget / Community Budget

This will give you an ROI number you can be proud of and continue to show off.

In essence, the main message of this chapter is that you need to take control of telling your community story. Most community people are extroverts *in their community*, but genuine *introverts* in other aspects of their career. With a SaaS company, you have a ton of data to be able to tell your story, and I want to ensure that your company sees your community's value and recognizes the hard work you do. Only you can step up and share these wins — no one will do it for you. It's not enough to say you don't measure because you hate math, or it doesn't matter because no one asks. You are doing great things to advance your company — they need to know. It will also help you to achieve many of your goals and aspirations for your community and your career. Showcasing how you're having an impact is the path for more support and resources. I hope you're inspired to take the steps you need to really show off your success!

Chapter 12: Where am I?

I hope by now you have a good handle on selecting goals and maybe even a rough idea for a CARGO plan. But maybe you're stuck on how to build out your larger community plan. That's where this chapter comes in. Some of the questions we will help you answer include: How do you really know where you are in your community journey and where you need to go? What happens if you inherit an existing community? How am you doing vis-à-vis other communities?

I frequently hear this last one from new (and sometimes not new) community builders in the space. They want to know how they are faring compared to "others." On the surface, it seems like a simple business question. We have a community, and others have communities — so how are we doing comparatively? What should our numbers look like?

I'm always concerned by this question. No two communities are alike. If we want our character and brand flavour to shine uniquely, does that make a comparison possible? I don't point this out to discourage measurement. Obviously, there are things to measure, benchmarks that could be tabulated, and general trends, but I don't want to focus on those here. Things change so rapidly, and each community is so specific. For this reason, I want to focus on the things you *should* be comparing yourself to.

To make the point clearer, let me compare looking at benchmarks like you would working on becoming a better runner. You don't worry about beating Usain Bolt in the 100M dash or even the several other competitors in that race. You work on running farther each time you run, or maybe you try to improve your speed or beat your personal record. The benchmark is your baseline, and a percentage increase or decrease of that initial number is what matters most. Worrying about an Olympic World Record time is not helping you get better. This is why you need to look at community benchmarks differently.

Some of you will tell me you still want to know how you're doing relative to your competition, but how does that really help you? Truly? Does that dismiss the excellent work you're doing? Each person, like each community, has their own circumstances. If you are improving, does that matter? How does obsessing what others do or don't do help you?

So back to community benchmark metrics and the first lesson: measure against yourself and your own improvement over time. The goal is continuous improvement. We also understand that you need to know where to anchor yourself. Sure, you can measure your progress, and make sure it's going up, but how do you know it's where you should be?

Welcome to the second part of benchmarking yourself. The best way I've found to do this is with a community life cycle model. However, unlike others, I wanted to focus on the behaviours a community should see in each stage (below is a copy).

As you will see, I avoid specific numbers, because I feel being tied down by them is a fool's errand. Every community is different, and more scientific people will pay attention to numbers and not the healthy positive and encouraging behaviours. Please also note, you don't need to satisfy every item on this list, but rather, aim to level up the community behaviours.

	DEVELOPMENT	INTRODUCTION	GROWTH	MATURITY	DECLINE
Phase Indicators	The concept of an online community is the solution to identified business problems. The concept is not yet defined, nor is the audience.	Launch of your online community to the public, with a core group of fans, influencers or selected customers.	Your community is open to the public and you are beginning to identify potential moderators, brand ambassadors, things are growing organically without day to day watchfulness.	Community manager is not involved in the day to day, but focused on policy and general tone. Managing the moderation team/ community team is the main focus.	Traffic is declining, there are many uncommented discussions appearing, and active user numbers are dropping.
Key tasks	Survey of potential audience, identification of key stakeholders internally. Identify the type of community you are trying to build - main focus: Support, Product, Ambassador or Network (S.P.A.N)	Identifying who can be your core launch group. Assure organizational resources. Platform structure, settings, gamification levels are implemented at a basic level. Soft launch to test assumptions and iterate.	Identify and nurture key contributors, and moderators. Maintain consistent level of content production. Ensure community culture and norms remain consistent with the influx of new members. You are regularly exceeding your community goals.	Managing the moderation team to continue to ensure consistency. Ensure your organization is aware of your contributions. Involving the community members in your larger business - introducing them to other departments. Optimize, test, and continue interesting to stay relevant.	Time to reinvigorate, interview your community, comm-unity refresh (new design), community manager need to get more involved in the day to day.
Graduating Task	Create a plan (See C.A.R.G.O), which includes a clear concept, how you will acquire and retain community members and finally how you'll measure success for your goals and outcomes. It should be metric driven.	You've launched, tweaked your categories, gamification system and your team have opened up your community to the larger public - full launch. Hit initial baseline goals consistently.	You're identified brand ambassadors. You have trusted moderators. You are ready to select another letter from S.P.A.N to complement your original choice. Community cultural norms are being enforced by the members with little interaction from you or your team. You are continually meeting community goals in a predictable way.	Guard against falling interest, by ensuring you are innovating, listening to your audience, and doing more of the stuff they like, iterating and growing the community culture, to the point of self-sustainability.	Complete refresh, reconnection of the CM to the community, and seeing positive metric signs of increased participation ratio of discussions to comments at a better level.
Team Composition	* Community Manager	* Community Manager * Staff assistance	* Community Manager * Moderation team from staff/community * Ambassador program	* Community Management Dept. * Minimal staff involvement * Moderation from community * Solid ambassador program	* Community Manager * Staff assistance
Executive Involvement	Budget for project assured.	Executive sponsor in loop on activity.	Regular reporting to the executive team - interest in the community and impact of decisions.	Community management is part of the executive team - or executives are hyper aware/ sensitive to community.	Lack of executive interest needs to be turned around.
Key Leading Indicators	Time spent outreaching/ Number of outreaches per day.	Number of resources created/Number of threads started by admins.	Number of threads started by community members.	Ratio of Comments to Discussion/ Number of Community Manager Interventions.	Number of threads started by admins/ Ratio of Comments to Discussion.
Key Lagging Indicators	Community Interest	Community Member Growth	Community Contribution Growth/ Community Member Growth	Community Satisfaction Scores	Community Member Growth/Community Satisfaction Scores
Timeline (approx)	• 0 to 2 months	• 1 to 3 months	• 6 to 48 months	• 48+ months	n/a

I hope the chart will assist you in plotting where you are on the life cycle spectrum, which is the only benchmark that matters. Let's break down the chart headings:

- Phase: Where are you in the life cycle?

117

- Key Tasks: What are the things you should be concerned with, or be doing?
- Graduating Tasks: What are the things that indicate you are on the way to the next stage?
- Team Composition: What is the makeup of the community team?
- Executive Involvement: Who in the org, at the executive level, is involved (if any)?
- Key Leading: Things you can watch as they happen and react to.
- Key Lagging: Things you can only see after the fact and change.

Let's now dive deep into the key indicators, how to identify where you are, and the graduating tasks to know you are on the way.

Development

This is the easiest to determine life cycle phases, but the hardest for someone new with no experience. You are in a stage where the concept of a community is just a twinkle in your eye. This is where those "we have a problem, and maybe the community could help" discussions pop up. You are in the crosshairs, maybe as the person who now has to shepherd this project.

Sometimes, though, you may be in a position where you are screaming and yelling (obviously, only in your head). You know a community could solve the problems, or be a beneficial asset to the company, but you don't know where to start. However, despite your eagerness, you now have the task of making the case, like a lawyer for the community, getting skeptical stakeholders on-side, and securing a budget.

This is where the CARGO plan can show your company that you're thinking strategically, hyper-focused on the company problems, trying to have an impact on company goals, and providing a definitive outcome. It's vital to get the goals right.

You will exit this phase when it becomes clear that an online community is the correct answer to solve your challenges, you've got a solid concept, and your CARGO plan is well-defined.

Key Indicator
The concept of an online community is the solution to the identified business problem(s). The concept, however, is not yet defined, nor is the audience, but you will begin to answer these questions.

Questions to Identify This
- Do you have a problem you feel a community can solve?
- What is the concept of your community?
- Have you tested this concept/idea with your potential membership?
- Do you have a set soft-launch date?

Graduating Task
Create a plan (see CARGO in previous chapter), which includes a clear concept, how you will acquire and retain community members, and finally, how you'll measure success for your goals and outcomes. It should be metric-driven.

Introduction
I like to think of this part of the journey like making a cake. In the previous phase, you got all the ingredients to make a

great cake. In this phase, you've made the batter, you've poured it into your pan, and you've placed it in the oven. It will end with you tasting the cake. If it's tasty, you keep going. If it comes out raw, tastes horrible, or is "missing" something, you need to experiment until you get it right and try again. Maybe the concept didn't stick in the end, or perhaps you didn't get enough traction with initial users.

At this point, you likely have your platform selected, and you are working on setup/settings and workflows. You have some people, hopefully, who will be supporting you and your customers/fans/clients, who are ready to open the community with you. They are giving you feedback on things to improve and support as needed to make it happen. You're all in for the ride and have a launch list ready (more on this later).

Now, if you're coming from another platform — as part of migration — see this phase as introducing the new environment. It's an exciting time, but a critical time to get your community on your side. It involves tons of communication, and their involvement, even before the migration. You want them to feel part of the process, and they need a way to share their opinions. Even if their ideas aren't used, you need to acknowledge them and explain decisions.

I have also seen well-planned migrations bring the community closer, because it's such an exciting time. I should add that this does not need to be a platform change either. It could simply be a significant refresh, or upgrade, that modernizes the look or enables new features, making the experience more welcoming.

You have exited this introduction phase with a public launch, and you've consistently hit your initial baseline goals. What is a baseline goal? It's whatever you determine as the first door of your success with your internal stakeholders. It could be, for example, that, typically, your support team receives 100 tickets a week. You start to see traffic in the forums increase, and boom, tickets drop to 80 tickets three weeks in a row. Customer satisfaction numbers are up, and call wait times are down.

And let's be clear with that example; it was just for illustrative purposes. The primary objective is the following: Has the community started to impact the organizational needs and goals identified? It's up to you and your team to determine what works best. You can move on to the next phase when you've got the recipe right and you see the beginning of impactful results.

Key Indicator
The focus is the launch of your online community to the public with a core group of fans, influencers, or selected customers.

Questions to Identify This
- Is the majority of your content in your community seeded content?
- Do you have categories created, but are they still flexible to change if needed?
- Do you have defined goals and KPIs you are measuring?
- Within your organization, is there interest/excitement in the community project?

Graduating Task
You are at full launch, hitting initial baseline goals consistently. Categories are tweaked as needed, your gamification system is mapped, and your team has opened up your community to the larger public.

Growth

This is one of the most fun and nerve-wracking stages. Your community is growing, and you've got tons of work, but you are continually exceeding your goals. You've got lots of new content created by your community members, and your ambassador program is engaged.

You may also be considering adding staff, and of course, the question becomes, how many moderators do you need? I will share more on moderation teams later, but as a spoiler to this question, the answer is, unsurprisingly, it depends. There is no magic formula for how many moderators you need. Sorry. I wish I could tell you that you need an extra moderator for every 10k page views, but it doesn't work like that. So how can you know how many you need? It's not as hard as you think. The answer is, have as many moderators as you need to accomplish your tasks. Do you heavily moderate the community because you have lots of trolls? Do you need weekend coverage? Do you need holiday coverage? Do you have an active group in another time zone while you sleep? Add moderators, slowly, and accordingly, and make sure you read the chapter on choosing moderators too.

In this phase, the tendency you need to guard against would be falsely assuming you've arrived. I have seen too many communities falter after some time because a new community manager thinks the job is done or that they can go on cruise control. Don't get me wrong. Please enjoy the moment. Take the pat on the back, but also realize that this is a crucial time to ensure your community culture and tone continue with their initial purpose. This becomes essential as the influx of new blood rushes into your cozy little space.

The growth phase is also where you can start to consider adding to your SPAN selection. For example, imagine you are a well-oiled support community. Now you will add aspects to help product teams with ideation, product feedback, and user interaction with product management. To be clear, in larger companies, they can manage more than one SPAN at a time, because they generally invest in the teams to handle it — and it's not on the shoulders of one individual.

The growth phase ends when you consistently meet your goals, and the other key metrics become the norm — or almost expected. In other words, no sustained surprise spikes or over-exceeding internal benchmarks by leaps and bounds. Some companies run right through growth into the next phase. However, some communities stay in growth mode for longer.

If you have an existing community that has migrated, the growth phase could be short, but there could also be a massive spike. No two communities are alike, so just enjoy the ride. You'll know when you hit the next phase, trust me.

Key Indicator

Your community is operating, and you are beginning to identify potential moderators and brand ambassadors. You can look to add other SPAN areas. Things are growing organically, for the most part, from member content.

Questions to Identify This
- Do you see continuous growth toward your goals and KPIs?
- Are you adding head count to your team?
- Are you developing, or have you developed, a path for moderators to volunteer?

- Are you developing, or have you developed, an ambassador program?

<u>Graduating Task</u>
You've identified brand ambassadors. You have trusted moderators. You are ready to focus on the next letter from SPAN to complement your original choices. The members are enforcing community cultural norms with little interaction from you or your team. You are continually predictably meeting community goals.

Maturity

This is when you enter the "predictable and consistent" phase. You are not necessarily taking your foot off the gas, as much as you are turning more to the team's management and overarching strategy. You've got things figured out. The focus is on another dimension your community can handle (as mentioned above , adding ideation, for example, to your Q&A community).

It's also about ensuring that things continue to run smoothly. Think of it like this: I am sure the first McDonald's made great hamburgers. They were probably so tasty. Then franchise happened, and then they needed to replicate and make sure the meals were consistent. Now we debate all kinds of things about the health or taste of McDonald's, all these years later, but you cannot but stand in awe of the fact that you can have a similar experience in Montreal, as you will have in Paris or Amsterdam. Sure, the names of the burgers may change for local language, or the sides might be different, but a Big Mac is a Big Mac. They have a procedure and a handbook to ensure uniformity. However, underneath it all, the success comes from the strict adherence to "The System."

So, where am I going with this analogy, you ask? As you step further away from the day-to-day and rely on others, you want to ensure consistent quality. Have you created your "system"? Is there a handbook of what to do in specific scenarios? Do you have a process in place to ensure moderators are consistent in applying the rules? Are there regular check-ins with this team? At the maturity stage, you should already have this in place. Preferably, you've done this early on, but I know sometimes the growth curve can make things so busy, that putting the systems in place is one of the hallmarks of maturity. Going back to the McDonald's example, it's not about getting out as many sandwiches as you can, but about creating that consistent quality experience. I have seen (and created) so many of these documents. We will delve into building your own in a later chapter. As you will learn, they are essential operating manuals infused with the unique elements of your community.

Can I also say that I hate the word "maturity," in many ways, for the connotations associated with it? Some think it means you're boring or stale. This is not at all how we should look at this stage. This stage is fun. You've arrived. You've placed structures, feedback systems, and things can mostly run without your constant supervision into every element, and it also means a lot of the community is self-sustaining.

At this stage, content is being created by the community, and your staff or employees should be almost able to melt into the background. Look at how things happen within the Apple product or Google Advertising online communities. It's so rare that their team will pop in — if ever. This is the moment you've arrived at maturity.

However, this can also be the most dangerous. The most significant risk at this point is complacency. This is also where you have to guard against people in your organization thinking the community project "is complete." A community is a living organism. You see, just like a plant, a community can continue to live without much involvement if it gets rain and sun. However, the owner still needs to check in, so pests don't eat those lovely plants unabated. So as much as you can step away, this does not mean you can ignore it.

Key Indicator

The community manager is not involved in the day-to-day, but instead, focused on policy and general tone. Managing the moderation team/community team is the main focus.

Questions to Identify This

- Is the community content machine more or less self-sustained by user generated content?
- Is the team more focused on analytics reports and general policy enforcement?
- Do you have a solid core of moderators and brand ambassadors?
- Is the community considered an essential channel for your company?
- Are you maintaining the goals/objectives for the community?

Graduating Task

Guard against decreasing interest, by ensuring you are innovating, listening to your audience, and doing more of the stuff they like, iterating and growing the community culture to the point of self-sustainability. If the community is being taken for granted and ignored by the organization, you are in peril.

Decline

As I've mentioned above, I hate the word maturity because of the negative connotation. Well, I hate the word "decline," but I've adopted the commonly accepted terms used for the product life cycle. We should really consider this the "time for renewal" phase.

My hope is that you identify this sooner rather than later. I will also not pretend, or tell you, that all communities in decline can be saved. I also wish I could give you an exact formula on the work needed to turn things around, but as a rule of thumb, consider the difficulty of reversing decline as being directly correlated to the amount and length of time the community sat in neglect. If your company abandoned your community, or it's been a ghost town for years, it can be tough to convince people to come back or even trust you.

The beginning of the renewal of your community should start with a good dose of listening to those in your community who are still around, or tracking down those who used to be keenly involved. Keep in mind that hearing and listening are not the same. The difference is simple. Hearing is simply the action of your ear reacting to sound waves. Listening is being present, asking open-ended questions, and really showing you care. Most important is taking action and doing something with the information.

Brainstorm with the team or on your own. Do you have the capacity for the investment to turn things around? Do you have the energy? Do you have the budget/resources?

If the answer is yes, it's about building internal excitement and a deadline. Now I am not saying this because I currently work at a vendor, but because I always believed it. It does not necessarily require a platform migration, as much as it may require a software upgrade, attention to new features, a new design, a reorganization of content. This is why it's so crucial to give yourself a deadline — a date to aim for.

I should also add, when you choose this "relaunch" date, make it a good constraint goal that pushes you. Don't fall into the trap of something far off, like the "end of the year." By the end of the quarter is a nice goal. Or tie it to a big event for the company. Something that gets people focused, and then you can use it as a springboard for the relaunch.

You will need to involve your marketing team deeply. Trust me, they will enjoy this, and so will you. It's about hitting those emotional triggers and personas to help drive your community back to your platform. Getting visibility to your new community will be just as important as the creativity of how you do it.

In this phase, you may need to find an executive sponsor and, hopefully, get internal support to assist you in the relaunch. You will want to start acting like you are in the introduction phase. It's go time! This is your chance to resurrect something that, hopefully, becomes special.

Key Indicator
Traffic is declining, many uncommented/unanswered discussions are appearing, and active user numbers are dropping. No one has cared or managed the community for a serious length of time.

Questions to Identify This
- Is there little to no excitement about the community within your organization?
- Are you finding there are days when no one posts or there is no activity in your community?

- Are page views, time on site, and other key traffic metrics significantly down?
- Are you finding it hard to get support internally to make your community better?

Graduating Task
Restart and refresh. Reconnection of the community manager to the community and seeing positive metric signs of increased participation ratio of discussions to comments at a better level.

So, there you have it, the five phases of the life cycle. However, I do want to point out that your community may not fit neatly into one bucket. This is not an exact science, so be patient, and place your community where you feel it fits based on the descriptors. The goal is more to see if you need to push forward, maintain, or renew. These are the three paths you can take:

- You will push forward when it's new, in development, intro, or growth stages.
- You will maintain/improve at maturity.
- You will regroup/renew if you identify a decline.

Finally, I know some of you *still* want the numbers to benchmark. The reality is, most data is too specific to matter for your community, so do yourself a favour, and benchmark yourself against yourself and where you are in your community maturity journey. It's the most helpful and fairest thing you can do for yourself and your community!

Congrats on all the work you've done so far! Working from scratch can be hard. There are lots of things at the start to consider, and it's not always so linear or step-by-step. There are many considerations one needs to balance all at once. However, by this point, I hope you have identified your MVPs, selected a SPAN, create a solid

CARGO plan, and decided what platform to build your community. If so, you're ready to move forward.

It's crucial to remember that deploying community software is easy, but building a community and creating a community plan takes time. You are also allowed to adjust as you get new data and rethink things. However, don't fall into the trap of perfection. No one is ever perfect. I have seen way too many community launches suffer from trying to reach perfection before launch. Community-building never ends, so be open with your community that this is a process and be ready to adapt once things really start moving.

With this in mind, it's time for us to begin the path towards a soft launch. Don't worry, my friends, we will move slowly and ensure you have what you need in this next phase. Onward to the next chapter!

Chapter 13: Testing, Testing, 1, 2, 3 — Is This Thing On?

I was part of a team opening a huge restaurant in one of the most prestigious addresses in Montreal at the centre of the business district. We had a menu and equipment; however, we were not yet ready for the expected crowds. So, as is tradition, the restaurant opened the doors for a soft launch. One of our cooks went to place a pan on the burner to begin the first order. If I recall, it was a chicken fajita plate. There was no heat on the pan. Nothing. Why? They had installed a state-of-the-art (at the time) flat glass cooking area. Electricians were called, managers came running, all hands on deck, to find a solution.

We had just opened the doors, and our kitchen was at a standstill. After 30 minutes or so, it was realized that the pans they had tested on the stove during installation were different from the professional cookware we were using at launch. They had bought fancy, and apparently too light (in terms of weight), pans, which did not trigger the sensor. People were clamouring for food now, so the manager ran to a large kitchen equipment store and bought enough pans so we could make it through service. At the end of the shift, we made adjustments to extremely new (and, I should mention, expensive) cookware. Later that week, when we launched, the stove worked, and all those hungry businesspeople were well-fed for many, many years.

Blame my early career exposure to the restaurant business, but it left a lasting impression on me regarding the importance of a soft launch. You can think everything is ready, but the soft launch is where you get to see if it works in practice. Most importantly, it's better to tweak and find out, with a trusted early audience, what isn't working than with the general public, who may not be as willing to give you a second chance.

Now some of you may already have an existing community — or something you are inheriting. However, I would suggest that, if you are the new person in town, borrow some of the elements of the soft launch as you take over. It's a chance to put your mark on the community, build excitement, and I think, most importantly, show the community you care and want the best for them too.

So where to start? I don't want to be too prescriptive in terms of deadlines and timelines. I do want to give you an idea of the things to consider. The two bookends of this conversation are: "When is the soft launch?" and "When is the public (mass audience) launch?"

Let's start now with the soft launch. To map out this plan, I want to review my CARGO plan, the life cycle objectives, and the other conversations or interviews I've had (both internally and externally). Consider this part of the journey in this way: You are in a new blank apartment or house, you have a sense in your head of what you want, but now it's time to buy furniture and actually place it. In other words, we move to the tactical. Let's get designing!

What Will the Entrance Look Like?

The first consideration is how people will get in. Do you want everyone in at once? Do you want them to use Twitter social login? Do you have your own login system? The best-in-class way to do this is what is known as SSO. What is SSO, you ask? It stands for single sign-on. The idea or concept is that your company (probably) has an account system that your customers/clients use to deal with your company. The goal is to add your community to this system through a process called SSO, which can use a protocol like

OAuth or SAML to make it a seamless experience. You yourself may have been using SSO in most of your online experiences. Why not bring it to your space to build a community? The goal is to reduce friction and make signing up or signing in painless. No one wants two passwords (or more) to deal with the same business entity. Do everyone a favour and be the hero who makes this happen. This is a battle worth having for success.

Who's Coming to the Community?

The next thing to consider are the personas you've identified earlier in the book. You want to ensure every persona you are targeting has something. This means using your community technology to segment them, or showcase different content. Maybe not all areas of the community need to be accessible to everyone. Use your community technology to determine permissions (preferably using that SSO) and the business case you have identified for its existence. This is also where you can start to create broad themes for categories.

What Categories Should I Create?

I always recommend you start with broad categories and grow from there. Creating too many categories can lead to "post-paralysis," where people are unsure where to post things, and then your moderators spend all their time moving discussions.

So how can you know what basic categories to start with? Use the categories from your website. Look at a competitor's community and what their more prominent areas are with the most traffic. Look at the search history. Talk to your support or CSM teams. Even ask your customers for ideas. There are many people who can help you be inspired.

One suggestion about a category I love, but which needs some careful thought, is a "Welcome" category. Consider this a spot for helping people understand how to use the forum platform or your product. Almost like an onboarding category.

I am not a big fan of the introduction threads, not because I'm an asshole — I love people. However, while these always start with admirable intentions, I notice they eventually become vast wastelands where people just go through the motions. Consider categories like "What Are You Working On?" or "Share Your Project" instead. Those give people something concrete to engage with.

Be careful with the "General" category. It's fine to start with, but make sure, eventually, that it goes away. The General category should be a testing ground, helping you sculpt the right topics or niches into more specific categories. Broad categories invite the kinds of conversations you may not want to encourage later on — because it's so general. Later, you may wish to create a "Water Cooler" or "Café" category, where you allow conversations about the weather, sports, or other things. It's at your discretion and the level at which you can monitor these areas with your team. These categories are great for people building connections and fostering that sense of community. It certainly can't be all work all the time, but only you can decide what makes sense for your audience.

Can We Clean Up the Existing Spaces?
For those with existing communities, you may want to consider pruning, organizing, or archiving categories. However, big caution, friend. Do this in consultation with the community, with transparency of plans. Especially in large communities, specific categories (or topics) have their

own meta communities, so it's best to involve them. Also, be careful from an SEO perspective. You don't want to kill off areas that drive people to find you. I am a big fan of switching to read-only, rather than deleting.

What Features to Consider?

The next consideration will be forum features, but don't go feature crazy. Which software features do you need to turn on or modify to make the experience amazing? What features are in line with the personas and the business objectives? For example, do you plan to give badges to founders to excite and reward these special people? Do you want to turn on the Q&A plugin so you have a space for new people to ask questions? Do you need to turn on an ideation plugin to create an area for people to make suggestions for your product team?

Remember, you don't need to turn all features on now, nor should you. Get the bits you need to make things feel like home, just like when you got your first apartment. Having a bed and a place for your clothes was important. Accent tables, rugs, and vases could wait, although they would come — we all know — at some point.

For my friends here with existing communities, this can be the time to review features and pare back those that don't make sense. Maybe you have blogs for every member, and two people use them, but the moderation effort does not make sense. There are other ways you can give those two people a (better) outlet, such as allowing them to create featured content — giving them a more prominent space in the main community.

What Content Do We Want Them to Read?

Next, we will need to consider content. For the new community, the persona information should guide you. I like to create a worksheet with each persona, when I expect them in the community, and the content I need to have in the community from them to feel at home.

This is the idea of "seeding content," which you may have come across. The idea is to get the conversation going. It should be something with a direct POV or that requires people to provide their perspective. So instead of asking "Do you like product X?" you will want the question to be "What do you like best about product X?" or "What advice would you give someone using product X for the first time?"

There are other ways to find topics to discuss. Here are just a few:

- Google Trends: Look at terms people search for, or which are related to your topic, by region.
- Suggested search terms: In Google or Bing, you have auto-suggestions on keywords, but you can also see related search links. These may be great topics.
- Be inspired: Do competitive research on what other communities in your space are seeing massive conversation around. Research forums, comments, or blog articles for this information.
- Examine data: What pages on your website drive traffic? What do people search for on your website? Your analytics tool should have the info, and if not, the Google Analytics tool is free and easy to set up to find this info.
- Talk to people: Ask the experts what areas to learn about or their predictions for future trends. Ask your sales and support teams what the common questions are.

With hope, these five ideas get your creative juices going for content, but what do you do with it now? As a young community manager, and for those without experience, it seems like a sock puppet is a great idea — as I did myself early on. If you don't know what a sock puppet is, you're probably still aware of the concept. This is a (wrong) tactic where you create a made-up account to ask questions (the "sock puppet"), and then proceed to answer or talk to that "person," as though they were real. Think of it like a ventriloquist and their dummy. Sure, you can have a conversation, but it is empty. Worst of all, what happens as time goes on and that sock puppet stops participating or someone tries to interact with them?

I know it's tempting to create fake accounts, but please don't do it. There are a couple of other ways you can handle this that are much more ethical. Here is one of my personal favourites:

Create one profile, specifically noting it is "not human" on the profile page. Indicate that you will be sharing and starting conversations from other sources, and welcome people to chime in. You then invite *real* people in your company or people in your early launch group to add their answers. The point is to be transparent and authentic. No one will blame you in a brand-new community for having some starter content. You do need it. Otherwise, this will be like a high school dance, where the boys and girls stare at one another, waiting for someone else to dance first. Make it easier on everyone by already dancing with your close associates.

Hopefully, your team members, either in marketing or product, can assist in writing up some content. If not them, there are others who can help. Consider reaching out to your launch core group or passionate customers. If you can't get anyone excited or caring to talk in the community, fake accounts are not the solution. Your community concept is the problem.

Assembling Your Community Launch Core Members

I briefly mentioned it before, but this is also when you should be identifying your core members to help you with the launch. You want real people, who have an interest in the topic and who are willing to provide feedback. These people can also volunteer topics or posts to start the conversation. You can reward these people with a founder's badge, and they should be real people from your audience.

You may have talked to these people in the discovery phase, or identified them with the help of your team. These can be your company's customer advocates. Additionally, you might have a goal for each CSM or sales rep to recruit one customer champion. The objective is to find representatives from the audience you are aiming to attract. They will be key guiding lights from the beginning.

The soft-launch phase is about testing and sussing out what will have the best impact on you and the community. This initial audience should be composed of fans and staff. It does not necessarily need to be staff involved in the community project, but those who are interested in the community *subject*. You'd be amazed how many times someone in a support role or someone junior in the organization will have a lot of eagerness to be involved in a community project. It's an excellent way for them to learn about the company, the product, and the team, and to be more involved for their careers.

It's also important that this group should not include your friends or family. It's a bad idea. Returning to my fascination with restaurant soft launches, there is something from this industry that you should *never* copy. This is the trend in the restaurant industry of doing soft launches with only friends and family. Maybe part of it is a way to say thanks to your family and friends for being supportive as you've been stressed and hard to reach during this time. However, this is a horrible idea for your community launch group. In a restaurant setting, people eat, so it can be a broader audience. With a community, it's imperative you have the right, and specific, people.

If you've done your planning right, and gotten your personas down correctly, then you know roughly who the community is for. Those are the people, or people like them, who you want to have for your soft launch. Now I know you may have close friends or family in those roles, but please skip them from the soft launch. I know your dad, mom, sister, or best friends might mean well, but it will be a rare case that they can give you good, honest advice, even if they are an active customer of your company. The same goes for friends outside the industry or the focus of your community. You need to talk to your audience. You can undoubtedly get opinions from friends and family, but don't make any significant judgements on content, process, or plan without validating with your audience.

How to Find Even More Early Members

Maybe you're struggling to find some core members. Here is a method to connect with a potential audience when you are struggling. Find your target personas on LinkedIn via search. Send a nice personalized and professional email, ensuring you explain what's in it for them if they help you. Don't be saddened if you get no replies or even if you get rebuffed. However, I think a well-constructed, polite email about a new project, especially targeting their needs properly, is something they will respond to.

This is the key: proper messaging. Not sure what to say? Look at the discovery interviews you did to make your CARGO plan. If you're still unsure, maybe your marketing friends can help. Just please don't do mass generic emails. These don't work for what you need.

Once you get a response, book a meeting. Have a conversation around the concept of your community and the content that intrigues them. You can also ask them if they'd be interested in helping you build such a space and providing you with feedback.

Another way to identify this group is through your support team or customer success team. They likely know who the passionate and interested people will be. Have them introduce you to them and involve them in the process.

Have some fun with this group you create. You can give it a fancy name like Community Council and have a weekly 30-minute call to talk about the issues or ideas as you build out your space. The real point is to talk and involve people who would use the community as early as possible and get the stage set (so to speak) for the more significant launch that's coming.

What About Existing Communities?

A soft-launch mindset for an *existing* community is really a relaunch. It's a chance to shake things up for the community — in a good way — and tell them you are here, listening, and planning to make positive changes.

I briefly sprinkled in some tidbits for an existing community in the previous pages; however, the overall tactics will likely differ for you. It comes down to embracing the existing community and over-communicating. A relaunch is easier because you already should have an audience to help in some ways. The main challenge you will face is that most people hate change, even if, in the long term, it's better. However, if you have decided a relaunch is needed after talking with key community people, don't be scared of the hard things. You may also be surprised. Some communities are more adaptable to change than others, but I also believe having proper preparation can mitigate most issues.

The first thing I like to do is identify or create a "community booster club." Now, this can be something official or ad hoc, but you need to know the people in the community you can rely on or trust. These should, hopefully, be people with a positive attitude, who can think of the greater community's needs. You should discreetly reach out to them as early as possible and let them know change is coming and you'd like their support. Bringing them in, with this special advance notice, will hopefully encourage their support.

The next step, as soon as you can, is to communicate endlessly. Your boosters may be excellent, but in my experience, secrets don't last forever, so don't wait too long to share with the rest of the community. Over-communication makes them feel part of the process. Also, give them a chance to voice their concerns and provide opinions on the things you can.

You can create a section in your community about the changes coming. There are some considerations regarding that too. I like to make sure it's not the first category people see, so I tend to make it the last category in the tree, so it's not the immediate experience for new people. I have also seen it be a restricted category for accounts of a certain age. Only you know what will work best for your community.

Whatever setup you choose, make sure your communications include:
- Why is a relaunch needed?
- What will the relaunch process look like?
- How can the community participate?

- What's the timeline, if you know that?

Have an honest and open dialogue, with promised updates at set intervals, if possible — like a monthly "state of the community" post. At the very least, create some mechanism by which people within your community can share their feedback. How can they communicate what they like or don't like about the community? Also, how can they share what they want to see? Making them part of the change is crucial to their acceptance, even if you can't deliver on all the things they hope for.

Another aspect of the relaunch is wearing your editor's hat. What content/ elements/categories of the community will or will not come to the other side? Maybe a low-traffic category will be left out. Perhaps you'll decide that personal blogs are no longer needed. Make sure these changes are communicated, why the decisions are being made, and offer alternatives, if possible. For example, if a category has low traffic but a passionate base that does not coincide with your new concept, maybe create a social group within the platform for them.

The essence of any relaunch review is about trimming the community. It's time to get rid of the things that no longer make sense or drag down the health of the community. It's about pruning and care, so your community can go forward and grow with your new plans in mind. Huzzah!

I'm glad to have gotten your mind spinning with ideas, but now I need to pin you down with the most crucial aspect of any launch. It's time to commit to a date on which you will (re)launch your community. It's essential to have a date. Not some random imprecise target. It should be taken seriously, and everyone throughout the organization should be aware.

This pre-soft-launch period is the crucial on-ramp to the soft launch. You are likely doing your best duck impression — calm on the surface, with legs just working so hard to stay afloat. While some companies are lucky to have special people to rely on in this phase, it's also just as common to be alone or have limited resources. Don't stress yourself out. Do the best you can. The goal of the soft launch is to make sure you have a functional space. Hopefully, it can help you attract the help you will need. This is why I need to stress: Things don't need to be perfect. Don't allow the drive for perfection to impede your launch. Communities grow, things change. Your aim is to construct the scaffolding of the building. What you need for the soft launch is enough to try out the concept, ideas, processes, and workflows. The look, feel, and extra features can come over time.

Okay, let's just take a pause here and review some of the things you should be working on before soft-launch doors open. This is the time to fine-tune any and all workflows you've created and what people will experience. Some of the things you want to consider:

- How easy is it to find the community?
- How easy is it to sign up?
- Is the registration form confusing?
- What happens after a new user signs up?
- What happens in the coming days?
- How do we capture what happens?

Now the above list is important for your soft launch, but it's also a list I would argue is super important on a *relaunch*. So many times, I run into a leaky bucket — something that was changed by another department, that you didn't know was impacting your community. For example, I recall one company I was working with that launched after spending a ton on social media advertisements to get their audience involved in the community content. The people were clicking the ads, but they just were not showing up in the community. When I audited the sign-up experience, we determined that members were being redirected to the wrong spot after registration. Without communicating to the community team, someone had changed the redirect upon community registration to a purchase page for software. Even after signing up for a software demo to get past that page, the potential member was sent into a series of other pages. They *never* got back to the community. If we had not done the audit, we would have found out too late. Thankfully, the audit saved us. Once we fixed it, things started to hum back to life.

This is why the soft-launch stage is so crucial to test, get feedback, modify, and test again. Indeed, you will have taken your best guesses on what works, but this is the time to test your assumptions. I'm also a big fan of using tools like Crazy Egg, Hotjar, and other analytics tools that look at behaviour. Where are people clicking? Where are people getting stuck? How do we solve that? Make sure your analytics code is working the best it can before you open the doors. Lots of analytics solutions only work on the data once enabled, so you won't be able to go back in time.

Community Mission and Community Guidelines
Another thing to consider is refining or defining the community culture through your mission statement and community guidelines. The mission should come naturally from the CARGO plan on the concept you've selected. It will help you determine who the community is for and who it's not for. This should also help in the creation of the community guidelines.

Community guidelines are super important, but they are also very community-specific. I could write a separate book on this, but I will leave that for another time. Instead, I will share some quick thoughts. I would look at what others in your space are doing with their community guidelines. I would also consider your audience. In this book, we are mainly focused on B2B communities. Because of this audience, something is working in your favour, which is a professional reputation. In general, people with a professional profile will behave. A good rule of thumb is to make the rules concise, as well as easy to read and recall.

Some of the rules you want to consider:

- Protecting any marginalized identity group from harassment and unwanted attention
- Zero tolerance for racism or hate speech
- Prohibiting attacks on other members and encouraging discussing ideas
- Cautioning that you can ban for any reason or remove any content, with or without notice, and that all decisions are final
- Prohibiting self-promotion or solicitation of member businesses
- Escalation procedures and who to contact to escalate an issue

Self-promotion is where I have seen most infractions in the B2B communities. Members will solicit or promote their businesses to others, so being clear that this is not welcome should suffice. If you want to allow this, one solution I have seen is to offer people a day, or an area, to post this information. However, I should warn you, this is not very engaging content. Personally, I don't bother doing this — but test what works for your community. In most online communities, a member profile will have their business information. If other members want to learn more from them, they can reach out via direct message (DM). I want to be clear, in this example, a *member is reaching out to them* privately. You should not allow a *business to solicit others* privately in your community without a member consenting to that. However, those are my thoughts on it. It's your community to do with as you choose, and each space is different. For example, there might be a space for self-promotion for electricians or plumbers looking for freelance work in a community for contractors.

When it comes to promoting one's work in a community, this is the advice I usually share with new members: When you join a community, place as much info as you can in your profile, and work on building a reputation within the community. It's amazing what happens when a member shares their expertise. Other members will quickly find them and reach out when needed. It happens all the time almost without fail.

My final thought on guidelines is that I can't tell you precisely what to write, because each space is unique. The main objective of your guidelines is to remind people to be respectful of one another and how to handle situations when they have an issue. You will need to consider what else makes sense for your community guidelines and match it to the space you want to create.

How to Use the Software Post/Area

One crucial piece of content you want before you launch is a "how to use the software" post or category. I don't say this only because I work at a software vendor, but because it often gets overlooked, and then your community members may miss out on really cool features you didn't tell them about. It also reduces frustration for new members who may not be familiar with the software you use or if the group is not as technical.

In my experience, the must-cover elements include the following: The editor used to post discussions in, any special features you may have enabled, any gamification elements (how to achieve reputation), how to bookmark/subscribe to content, how to send private messages (if enabled), how to manage notifications, and who to contact if there are any issues. Having this content is essential if you have made significant customizations to your platform or changed software. It's also helpful to get feedback from your selected group during the soft launch regarding what you need to expand on or include.

Building your Community Commitment Curve

I love the idea of the community commitment curve, especially during a soft launch, to visualize the paths we are creating for our members. My friend, Carrie Melissa Jones, really has written great stuff about it (and created a webinar) with Vanilla as the subject. I also know, not every community professional agrees with its usefulness. I guess you can tell how I feel about it. I think they're great!

However, I feel I've gotten ahead of myself without really explaining what it really is. So let me fix that. The idea of the community commitment curve is to plot out the asks you make of the people joining your community. The curve comes in as each ask takes more effort; however, as they complete these asks, it eventually gets them into a leadership role in the community. The end goal is to identify valuable members you can rely on in your community. It also helps you visualize if there are too many asks, or not enough, in each stage.

The commitment curve is also mighty, and in the wrong hands, can be abused. You've likely witnessed this in many mafia-type movies. A young man starts out by "delivering a package" for a local mobster. Then he gets a chance to drive the mob boss. Eventually, he's asked to participate in some sort of misdeed, like robbing a store. Finally, he is asked to kill someone in return for a more significant role in the "organization."

These are obviously not the kinds of communities we want to build, but I give this example as something you're likely to have seen. We want to develop *positive* asks, with value for the askee as much as the asker.

They can be simple asks, like signing up to the community, and they progress to asking a question, to answering a question, and so on and so on. This happens over four stages: Discovery, Onboarding, Engaging, and Leading

Plot out the asks at each stage, assigning an effort score (1 to 5). I have also created a handy sheet to help you map this out. Get a copy (and all the charts) at:

https://adrianspeyer.com/bk/files.zip

COMMUNITY COMMITMENT CURVE - CREATING AN MVP PROGRAM

Ask at			Ask at			Ask at			Ask at		
DISCOVERING	EFFORT 1-5	KEY KPI	ONBOARDING	EFFORT 1-5	KEY KPI	ENGAGING	EFFORT 1-5	KEY KPI	LEADING	EFFORT 1-5	KEY KPI
Visit the community	1	X	Create an account in the community	1	X	Comment on a discussion	1		Welcome a new person/ encourage them	1	
Follow your brand on social	2		Read the community guidelines	2		Join a social group	2		Report a post with concrete thought	2	
Read your blog/ knowledgebase	3		Bookmark a discussion	2		Create a discussion	3		Report a post for spam	2	
Subscribe to your newsletter	4		Follow a category	2		Ask a question	4		Answer a question correctly with links to your content or community content	3	
			React to a post	2		Actively participating in conversations (1-2 discussions per week, 3-4 comment a week)	5	X	Create original and useful content for the community	4	
			Update their profile with photo	3		Mention an expert in the community who can help	5		Write a knowledgebase document	4	
			Respond to your welcome emails	4					Manage a social group	4	
									Made rank level MVP	5	X

148

My twist is to select a key KPI, a sort of stepping-stone to the next level, which you can track to ensure your curve is working.

This is not the be-all end-all of your community plan. It's really to help you visualize the journey and make sure you don't have dozens of big asks and no small asks. I am also a fan of breaking this down by personas of the people in your community. Our goal is to push people to commit to the community and to take on leadership. Although it's important to note that some people will never advance in the curve, that's fine too. Our goal is to ensure a fair and clear path for those who choose to do so.

For my perfectionist friends, please don't get stuck here. There is no perfect community commitment curve out of the box, especially in the soft launch. The goal is to have a rough plan you can test and tweak. To reduce missing the mark, talk to your members and potential members about what you could ask of them and how they feel about the effort required for those tasks.

For those with an existing community, doing the community commitment curve may uncover where you have too many high-effort asks and where you need to modify those asks to make the journey flow better.

With all the pieces coming together in the pre-launch, you can now consider the final preparation for the soft launch. Here is a quick checklist for those following along:

- Talk to the potential community members, create persona/segments.
- Create a select group to be part of the initial launch and provide some sort of reward/recognition.
- Communicate endlessly and involve your community.

- Create an area for feedback on the community and share developments.
- Test all workflows — walk through sign-up and features (initial pass).
- Create "about this forum" content, including how to use the software.
- Add your community guidelines.
- Develop a community commitment curve.

This is not an endless checklist, but the rule of thumb is to consider these things, even if not in the final state. At this point, you need to keep yourself open-minded, ready for feedback, and continuously testing and tweaking.

Also, one thought about software. I didn't want to get so technical on the pre-launch from a software point of view, because it's so varied. However, I would be remiss not to mention to use a staging environment, where you and your close team can try out ideas/features and other important changes before they get moved to the live environment. Even after a soft launch, it's always a good process to avoid a bad experience for your community.

Once you have your live site ready, we can start considering the second phase of a soft launch, which is where you begin to invite people in by cohorts. I like to start with those who will likely be most positive and constructive in their criticism, so we can prepare a proper culture for those who may be more anti-change.

The initial groups in this launch are an essential bulwark to build the community culture you want and foster that critical momentum. You need them as much, if not more, as your internal team for success. Make sure you make this a special occasion for anyone joining at this point. This could be a launch call, or a video chat, as you go live from a war room, where everyone in your team is together, so everyone feels part of it. I've always been a fan of making people feel invested in the success by doing these types of calls. Maybe a toast can be made, or donuts can be eaten. Or even fun little invites with some company swag to those in the community helping with this portion of the launch.

Having a dedicated chat tool is also something I recommend for this launch. It adds some excitement to the immediacy of the launch. It also creates a space where you can act quickly. Use your team's favourite tool.

The final piece of advice I will give you, at this point, is to breathe. If you have an excited and passionate community, you will get *lots* of feedback. Take a moment to enjoy the excitement and pace yourself, so you don't get overwhelmed. Usually, people want their feedback to be acknowledged quickly. Communicate clearly, and as transparently as you can, about timelines. Take the time to figure out when and if you can implement their feedback where it makes sense. My main recommendation is that you don't stay silent. Give regular updates on the community, in a particular space, for those helping you. It's also a bonus if you can publicly highlight those who helped with their feedback.

In the end, this two-part soft launch has essentially been a launch without the publicity. You've done a lot of work up to now, so it may be hard to keep track. Before we set a final public launch date, here is the list of things I would suggest you have completed:

- Allocating proper team resources (with defined roles)
- Creating a team space (for help from your company/moderators)
- Introducing yourself as community manager to the community – and the very least the top contributors

- Publishing forum "how-to" content
- Writing your community guidelines
- Seeding content/category setup, with identified segments in mind
- Outlining your community content plan by segment for at least the first quarter
- Setting up a feedback area for those who wanting to ask forum-related questions and get help
- Finalizing post-sign-up workflows and single sign-on (if you are using this)
- "Finalizing" your community curve — you can always modify, but have it near complete
- Ensuring appropriate website visibility so people can find you
- Testing, testing, testing — including forum software features and expectations.

It seems like a short list when you look at it, but there is undoubtedly much to do. I've seen people take a few months to do this, and I've seen people take a year. I would do my best to create a confirmed launch date so you don't fall into a horrible state of perfectionism which can cause "failure to launch." It's 100% inevitable that, once you launch, changes will happen. However, if you do the work noted in this chapter and involve people in your community, it will go a lot smoother.

In the next chapter, we will look at ensuring you have a solid community launch plan. If you've ever done a marketing plan, or worked on one, it's relatively similar. Don't panic if you haven't though. I promise I'll be with you every step on the journey, so turn the page, and let us begin — onto the launch!

Also, if you need to take a break, I understand. I'll be here when you are ready, so don't worry :)

Chapter 14: Nowhere to Hide — Let's Get Ready For The Ride!

Here's a secret — well, it's not really a secret, but it seems to mostly get lost when people look at other communities — they don't just launch and succeed. Strong foundations lead to success. I can tell with great certitude, and after participating in hundreds of community launches, they are more manageable if you've done the planning.

To help you prepare with your own launch, we'll now cover some of the basics of managing a community launch to ensure maximum success. For those with an existing community, I'll highlight the key differences between launching for the first time and migrating to a new space.

As an accidental community manager, now is the time to tap into your skills, especially if you've ever done a marketing plan. Don't freak out if you've never done one — or that skill is not in your wheelhouse — because what you'll need isn't *exactly* a marketing plan. It's not just about the 4 Ps (product, price, place, and promotion). Either way, I got you.

Essentially, we want to create a community marketing plan. What does that entail, you ask? It's a document that outlines how you and your marketing team will work *together* to tell the world your community exists. It will also be a clear document to tell your executive team what the heck your plan is — and show how serious you are! To be honest, you can use this even earlier in the process to get buy-in on your project, but after all the pre-launch work you've done, most of this should be easy to fill in.

I can sense trepidation in some of you. Please, don't worry. I'll take you step-by-step through creating your own community marketing plan. You can add the elements you need for your specific case, but let's review the sections I consider essential to include:

Executive Summary: Here's the thing, most executives are super busy, so they want the critical stuff up front, in an easily digestible format. This section of the community marketing plan should summarize the mission of your community, making a connection to how it will impact the critical areas of your business. You will make clear who the key people in charge of executing "the plan" will be, and finally, as a nice touch, I would add a SWOT analysis.

A SWOT analysis is a four-square table, where you outline the strengths, weaknesses, opportunities, and threats for your community project. Example:

Strengths	Weaknesses	Opportunities	Threats
What our community is/ will be good at. What our community likes.	What we want to fix. Where we lack, and what we could use help with.	If we execute as intended, here are the benefits.	Here are things that could inhibit success, including competition.

Community Initiatives: In this section, you should add the elements you learned while building with your internal MVPs in mind and as you crafted your CARGO plan. You want to clearly articulate the company initiatives that matter, how they intersect with the community, and the initiatives, goals, and metrics you will launch to achieve them.

Start with company initiatives in a list and then add elements, such as below:

Initiative: Create a Support Space

Description: We plan on creating a space for our members to ask questions, which will be our number one source for self-support.

Goal: To reduce the number of tickets and allow our support team to work on the more complex issues for our customers.

Measure of success: Deflect 25 percent of first-line support — calls, tickets, emails with common questions

Target Audience: In this section, you will clearly articulate the concept of your community. In other words, why does it exist, and who will it serve? It may even make clear who it does *not* serve. It's not a crime to make it not available for everyone or to not serve everyone. It's also 100% acceptable to start with a section of your community and expand over time. The other vital elements in this section will be who your community personas are. These will be complete personas, worked out with the marketing/sales team, so they can identify who the perfect people are for your community. Finally, in this section, you can also add any competitive analysis. For example: "Within our target audience(s), we expect to compete with the following communities/companies." Lay out what they do well, and what we can learn from to attract our audience.

Community Marketing Plan and Promotion

- **Community Program Strategy:** In this section, you can share your initial brand ambassadors, if you have any, and how they will interact in creating content. It's fine if you don't have any, though. This section should really give a sense of the content you've seeded and your plans for the coming quarter (at a minimum). It should be a clear list of what content you're planning, which elements apply to specific personas, and which resources you need.

- **Community Budget:** What will the costs be associated with content creation, events, or meetups? If this is early on, before you actually buy the platform, it could include the cost of the platform. It could also include platform modification costs or costs of dev work. The idea is to be transparent in the financial commitment you need to make your plan happen.

- **Promotional Channels:** We will explore this more in-depth later, but this is where you'll outline the internal and external channels through which you will promote the community — for example, company newsletter, website, social media — and what that entails and which personas you are targeting. Example:
  Company Newsletter

  Purpose of channel: *Customer Awareness*
  Persona: *Buyers*

  Support needed: *Marketing team to include community content in their newsletter*

  Metrics to measure success: *25 new signups from the newsletter*

As you can see, this is a very comprehensive document that brings together many of the things you've probably already spoken about but places them into something a bit more official. The next step is to take a calendar and a spreadsheet to mark down the "who" and "when." Be very clear who owns what, the expectation of what they will do, what they will need to share or communicate, and when they will do it. Work backwards from your launch date.

I think this would be as good a time as any to reiterate the importance of selecting the right launch date. Now some may disagree with me, but there are specific dates better than others for a big public launch. It depends on the type of community and concept. Considering we are focusing on B2B communities in this book, let's not launch on a Friday or on the weekend. Let's also not do it on a Monday or Thursday — people are busy getting started on a Monday and Thursday is workhouse day, prepping for the weekend (like Friday). This leaves Tuesdays and Wednesdays as the best days for community launches.

The final element is to avoid significant events or holidays that could impact your launch. Nothing is worse than spending all the time and effort preparing, and then having the community launch hit on the long Thanksgiving weekend, and then trying to get people to remember your community again. I personally have been a big fan of launches occurring from January to May and September to mid-November as the best times. I like to avoid the summer and the last six weeks of the year. Now your situation may be different, but these are my general thoughts. You will know your case better.

As you may have noticed already, I am also a big fan of to-do lists. It's how I keep myself on task. You may have a different way to do this. That's fine. Use the way that works best for you. Trello, Jira, or Asana are just some of the options available. It's not the tool that matters here, so much as getting the elements right.

For the rest of the chapter, I will share these elements for a new launch and then a relaunching/migrated community — jump to the section that's appropriate for you. You may also notice some repetition from earlier parts of the book, but I've done this to help formalize your plans in one spot. Let us begin with the brand-new community launch.

New Community Launch List

- Community Marketing Plan and Promotion Set: This includes who does what and when — as we shared above. It includes how you'll broadcast the news and who you'll invite. It also encompasses how your community fits into the whole ecosystem. For example, being linked from the main nav instead of being hidden in the footer. I can tell you community failure will be 100 percent guaranteed if people do not know your community exists.

- Team Space (For Help): How does your team communicate? Create a proper space for these conversations to happen. Share best practices and examples. I have also been a fan of a moderator-only category where you can share community policy and have your team ask questions. In terms of dealing with moderators on specific cases, where you think a course correction is needed, please do it in private, but we will chat about this in another chapter.

- Community Manager Intro: Let people know who you are. My favourite community manager introduction was by Margot Mazur when she introduced herself as the community manager of Wistia. She posted a one-minute video to the community. In it, she was hula-hooping and juggling, but also telling them about herself in a voice-over. It ended in a direct shot with encouragement to join the conversation. It was short and sweet, but it clearly showed off her personality and was very welcoming. Now I am not suggesting you need to do something similar, but think of how you will let people know who you are as we shared in an earlier chapter.

- Forum How-To Content: This can be a video, or it can be multiple posts. Knowing how to use the tool is crucial for ensuring people get the most out of their experience. It is vital to have some "how to use this forum" content, no matter the platform. Not everyone is at the same technical level. I would suggest you segment the content into basic and advanced information. The basic items might be how to use the editor and notification preferences. The advanced or forum-specific content might explain how ranks work or how one joins your fantastic super user program if you have one — or plan to have one in the future. Of note, if you use gamification, certainly tell people about the levels or kinds of badges available (maybe keeping a couple of surprises), but there is no need to break down the formula of what each action leads to a badge. Easter eggs are fun too.

- Community Guidelines: These should contain the mission and expectations of member behaviour to create a great community culture. It should be specific enough, but not overly filled with legalese that no one will ever read. You should cover what content people can share, what they can't. In B2B communities, I've found it helpful to add a note about not doing self-promotion, and when in doubt, to consult with the mod team first. Hopefully, you don't need to point out that nudity, mature content, illegal software, or sharing confidential info is not allowed in a professional B2B community. Still, I will leave this up to you and your best sense of your community. Finally, you should have a clear policy on any harassment or hateful conduct, including discrimination, hate speech, bullying, or targeted attacks. No one size fits all, so let your community mission and your culture guide you. I covered this in the previous chapter if you need more ideas.

- Seeded Content/Category Setup: If you have done your segments, you will have already created categories. Make sure there is relevant content for each — that is, make sure they are set to drive the conversation. Don't post as a made-up user. Make posts from yourself or encourage your initial core group to help start and answer initial conversations. I'm also very frugal when creating categories and allowing the community to determine what needs its own space. Consider each category as its own culture and avoid conversation paralysis by not making so many category options that people don't know where to start a discussion. This is why Vanilla has, by default, a view for new communities to start with discussions first. It was very controversial at the time, because, up to then, forums were always a category-first-only view. For me, I found it best to let the community guide your category creation — unless there are clear delineations, such as radically different items. For example, if you have a large company with hardware and software, you may want to start with those two large categories.

- Feedback Area: This ensures a clear place for people to leave their feedback, questions, or ideas related to your community. It should be the last category on your list. I have seen some communities with this at the top, but this is not the experience you want people to have, so place it as the last category in the list. It's also important that it not be a black hole. Please make sure you have a process to acknowledge and respond to feedback in a timely and concrete manner.

- Team Resources Allocated (Defined Roles): What happens when bad stuff happens? Do you have a moderator crisis handbook? What if the forum goes down? How can you send a newsletter to the whole community? Who can answer the most technical questions that come in? What happens when no one gets an answer after 48 hours? Before you launch, have an idea who you have to help, where to get help, and make sure it's communicated clearly with the community team. We will delve into this more in a later chapter.

- Post-Sign-Up Workflows: What happens after people sign up? Do they get a welcome email with targeted ways to join the conversation — or are they going into the vast void? What, if any, promotion of community content is happening? It's a delicate balance between providing information and annoying those who want to consume and not participate. Make sure you listen to your community (look at unsubscribe rates, or ask for feedback) and have that conversation with them.

- Finalize Community Curve: Marketing has the buyer's journey. Community people have the community commitment curve. We've talked about it earlier, but hopefully, by now, you're happy with it. It's not a document set in stone, but it should be well-formed.

- Test Test Test!: In the movie *Glengarry Glen Ross* (based on the play by the amazing David Mamet), Alec Baldwin talks about ABC — "always be closing." For community, it's ABT — "always be testing." You'd be amazed how things break, or how people forget what a new community member experience is. Make sure, before you launch, to create a brand-new account — or trusted colleague do it — and ensure everything you expect to happen does happen. Plan to do this at least once a quarter. At a minimum, check that your community is still visible where it needs to be and that the sign-up experience is how it should be.

The Relaunch/Migrating Community Launch List
Many of the elements in the prior section are for new communities specifically — thought they might be relevant as a quick check. Specifically, for the older communities, migrated or relaunched, here are some extra things consider:

- Baselines and Historical Data: Unlike someone launching from scratch, you have a trove of invaluable data that I implore you to capture before the relaunch. Too many times, people will switch platforms or assume they will have the data to go back to and then be surprised when they have none. The point of the historical and baseline data is to track your success. See your trends and make adjustments as needed. Historically, maybe you've needed more staff or moderation help around an event in August. That would be good to know. It's also an excellent way of making sure, if anyone inherits your community in the future, that they know this too. Make sure you have a document that contains that information, including what "typical" numbers are. This will also let you measure how you are doing with your relaunch.

- Forum How-to Content: Creating how-to content ensures your users use all the cool features you may have enabled as part of your relaunch. If you've changed platforms, this is really important. If you can create "this is how you did it, and this is how you do it now" content, it's even better. The goal here is to acclimatize people as quickly as possible to the new platform and make it feel like home. These kinds of touches are often overlooked, but in my view, crucial.

- Team Resource and Space: If you have an existing community, I hope you already have team resources and spaces for your team. It's a great time to review your guidelines and work with your team to ensure they have all they need. The worst time to plan how to deal with a crisis is during a crisis. It's so much better to have already prepared. What is the escalation chain? What are the resources available? What do you do when things in your moderator handbook are not clear? How is it updated, and who is responsible for doing so?

- Feedback Area: Just as I would expect from a new launch, you will want to create a place for feedback. We want to also ensure we have a process to engage with this feedback and close the loop. If you ask for their feedback, make sure you have a way to ensure they feel heard and responded to. Also, depending on your audience and community, you may wish to have a separate space for trusted/long-term members. Indeed, most feedback is valuable, but new members and existing members will have different needs and points of view. Remember that it's your community, so see how it goes, and change as it makes sense. I would suggest this separation if you think older members will react negatively toward changes and scare away important feedback from newer members. This brings me to...

- Cheerleaders/Boosters: Get ready to combat negativity on the new platform. There are angels in every community, who just radiate positivity. I am not suggesting blind loyalty, necessarily, but they default to "trusting" you (as the community leader) to do the best to fix things you can. Find these people and keep them close before the relaunch. While most times, a relaunch or a change goes smoothly, there's always an unknown factor of how people will react. You will also want to have straightforward ways of handling people who are "vocally" unhappy in the community. This does not mean you need to ban them. Look to create a process to make them feel heard that avoids them growing into a black hole of negativity, bringing your whole community with them.

- Appropriate Website Visibility: If you've had the "community does not work" or "our community sucks or is toxic" experience in your company history, I would not be surprised to learn the link to your community is buried on your website. However, if the relaunch is to be a success, you really should plan to bring that visibility back. I encourage you to have a set date and ownership of deliverables tied to this. Don't assume it will happen, and don't just add the link back. I would strongly urge you to engage your marketing team on a communication plan (i.e., how will you show and tell the target audience your community space exists). A relaunch is something exciting that the marketing team will be pleased to help you with. A good rule of thumb is that your community should get, at minimum, the same visibility as your social media accounts, if not more. You have much more control over your own channels, so it should be much more prominent.

- Refine Post-Sign-Up Workflows: Make sure that things still make sense if you've made tweaks to your community. It will be a poor experience if automated welcome emails go to outdated resources or are sent on behalf of someone who has left the company. Consider also ways to add newly created content and resources to the email and a way people can jump into the action and make an impact!

- Review the Community Curve: Just because you've always done something doesn't mean you need to continue doing it. I really like the community commitment curve (as I shared in the previous chapter). It's an excellent way for you to review what you ask of your members, ensuring you have the correct number of asks at each moment in the curve, and that you're still heading towards the most positive leadership outcomes.

- Test Test Test!: Testing is always crucial, as I noted above in the section for people with new communities. As someone relaunching, testing is crucial for you to ensure no surprises with any modifications you've made. You may cause more anger by making changes without talking to the members of your community. Having them involved is not a bad thing, but you always want to look at data. Sometimes people love a feature — or say they do — but don't use it.

  I'm also a big fan of A/B testing, if you can do it. This is where a segment of your audience sees something different than others do, and you can gather invaluable data on their interaction with that thing. There are many tools out there which will allow you to test these things in your community. If you get to this point of a relaunch, you should also consider the leading/lagging indicators to watch to ensure you are heading in the right direction.

I would like to take a small break from lists for a moment. Take some time with a note-taking device of your choice. Make a list of what you wish to improve, but don't just focus on design (more on that in a moment). Remember, just because you change platforms or have a new theme, this doesn't matter long term if you've built upon a weak plan or process. This is why there may be some repetition and me restating things, because it's just so darn important for your success. So really dig deep on the things not related to aesthetics that need to change. Come back here when ready.

UX and Community Design Choices

I've not really covered this topic up to now, but I felt I needed a bit more space in this chapter to cover it. Regardless whether brand new or relaunched, we need to consider the look and feel of your community. In this specific context, I am talking about the actual design choices you make. It can be so hard when you're not a designer or have no experience. Also, unfortunately, when it comes to design, everyone has an opinion. Anyone in marketing knows what happens when "design by committee" happens. A simple ad banner can take a lot longer. Some people don't like a colour, a font, or a shape, and before you know it, the poor designer is exasperated and leaves without consensus. To make things even more complex, add into the mix certain "community experts," who may tell you there should be a menu on the left or that the search bar should or shouldn't be somewhere on the page. In one case, a community I owned followed so-called expert advice and lost 50% of its monthly revenue. Once we switched things back, within days, revenue was back to normal. Frightening, I know. So how do you solve this without losing your mind?

There is a solution, my friends. This is why I am taking a bit of a pause in our rush to launch to talk about design. I know the conversation about the look of your community will happen at some point, so why not now?

Where to start? My solution is rigorous A/B and multivariate testing, heatmap click tracking, mouse tracking, and user testing. In other words, listen to the data. Test, measure, modify, and repeat.

Now some of you may be familiar with some of these tools, but for those of you who are unfamiliar with them, I'd like to give you a crash course and dive a bit deeper into each of these.

Heatmaps and Click Tracking

The idea of heatmaps is that a hidden overlay is added to your site, that only you can see. It will record the mouse movements and clicks on the pages tracked by a piece of code. When you log into your heatmap tool, the closer to hot dark red an element is, the more important it is for your audience. Usually, most heatmap tools also record how far people scroll, too, so you can see which content is even seen. For example, are people missing that important piece of content, or is the join button too far down the page? This data can be crucial in making the case for placements or even creative design elements. This can help arbitrate a discussion between something that may look cool but be confusing or distracting. In short, if the data shows behaviours that are concerning, keep it simple.

Mouse Recording

Mouse recording software does exactly what you think it does. It follows the user's cursor on the page and where they go. You can watch as the mouse hovers over a button and whether it then gets confused or it whether the button is clicked. Or maybe your login form is confusing. You can watch their whole journey on the site, from start to finish, or get aggregated data of all visitors. The first time I saw this kind of tool in action, I was wowed — it made me fall in nerd love. When I watched with the team to see how people interacted with our site, we cheered or jeered as we watched the mouse movements. Seriously, though, seeing the whole journey, in real time, down to the individual users, was eye-opening. We could see where their mouse went, we could see the hesitations, we could also see the clicks and other choices they made. We could then come up with assumptions to fix things and use different tools, as I shared earlier, to test those choices on the fly.

User Testing

This is something I became obsessed with after reading a fantastic book by Steve Krug called *Don't Make Me Think*. The concept is to create scenarios and have the user talk through what they are thinking and seeing, and also record their screen as they move through them. I have used this process numerous times. It starts by finding people in your target audience and asking them to perform specific tasks in your community, and seeing how they respond, while talking about their thought process. This is a great way to get context around their choices, because they will verbalize what they are thinking as they move around your community. This is the most laborious process on the list, because it requires more planning, along with writing out a script and scenarios to test. There are online services to help you with it, and it's by far the most in-depth of all the choices when it comes to gathering data about design choices. Your marketing team may already be using a service, which may make things easier to access, so don't be too shy to ask!

A/B and Multivariate Testing

The first time I learned about this was through a story about how Amazon would regularly test the colour of buttons at checkout — down to the proper shade of a colour. I spent a long time in the e-commerce space, where we tested tons of elements of the checkout process. In case you were curious, green buttons almost always will be used, because of the fact that green means "go." Now, this is not to say you should change, or need to change, the colour of buttons in your community. This is where A/B and multivariate testing comes in. With A/B testing, you can test having a blue (the control/original colour) versus a green (the alternative colour) "join now" button and see which one gets more clicks and conversions. The best testing tools out there will allow you to control which percentage of the audience sees the new version. For example, you can decide if it's only new people to your community or all your members. As you can probably surmise, a multivariate testing tool can apply more than two choices.

What you choose depends really on your needs and also audience size. Doing these tests can be challenging if you don't have a large enough audience to get statistically significant results. In plain English, this means the data may not be relevant if you don't have a large enough sample. If only 10 people come in, and seven people click the green button, the sample size is too small to make a decision. Once again, if you choose a great tool, it should have a confidence score, or a statistical significance score, available. Google has a pretty cool tool called Optimize for this, but there are many others out there. Find the one that works best for you. I should say, this is really nerdy stuff, though, and in most cases, you don't need to do this.

However, if you like to love data and want to get a bit more technical, this might be a cool experiment!

I hope the above was helpful, because I know I went a tad into the weeds. However, don't worry, as tons of books, blogs, and websites can help you go deeper on these subjects. Also don't think you need to learn all this now. It's certainly something much more advanced and for more mature communities. I just want you to know these tools exist, because then you can ask your marketing, or other business teams, if you can use those tools, as well — if a conversation turns to design. While things might take longer (or just as long as design by committee), at least you will make decisions that are data-based and not on the opinion of someone who just hates the colour blue.

Also, one final note about adding code: please make sure you update any terms of service about cookie tracking if you do use these tools. Check with your CIO or the appropriate person internally. You may also add a way for users to opt out of tracking, depending on your location and audiences served.

I think I mentioned before that the most successful launches always had lots of work up front. If I didn't, well, I've said it now. There is no "build it and they will come." *Do* sweat the details. Talk to your potential community audience; don't assume. And please, by all things holy, have a plan with milestones, including testing. Amen.

Once you are ready — and have absorbed all the above — we should finally talk about the actual launch day. Certainly, you have set the date, as I shared earlier regarding selecting one, but how do you make it something enjoyable and special for your community? I mean, you did plan for that, right?

This is a party, and your whole community is invited. Treat it as such. Mail out "save the date" cards to your potential community. Create a livestream of you "going live" and inviting your most important supporters. Have a nice banner at the office, which people can see when they come in, telling them it's launch day. Maybe leave cupcakes on the desk of your key support people. All I am saying is, do something special — and make people feel like they should care and be invested.

What are some other things I like to do or have seen be successful? Plan to have a "war room," where all the key players can be together on launch day, or turn on some kind of video system, so your remote team can be part of it too. Share photos of your "war room" on social channels. Leverage all your marketing channels to share the special day. When people come into the community on the big day, make them feel welcomed in a unique way. Maybe a special badge or a video welcome from your CEO. Apple does a great job of making people feel special when they release a new phone. On launch day, if you buy a phone, they have their crew ready to give you a high five on your way out. It's really something special to see. What will your experience be like?

The final piece of advice I want to give is the most important: Launch. Don't get hung up on perfection. Fear can be paralyzing, and some communities never get to launch. Make a date to launch and do your best to stick to it. Most importantly, while many launches can occur without any hitches, issues happen, and most people know this. The main thing is how you and your team respond. Your reaction to the problem is how you will be judged by the community. Do your best, communicate, and be transparent.

If you follow the advice in this book, I'm sure you'll do great! Go get 'em, rock star!

Chapter 15: Let's Talk SEO!

Forums are great for SEO (sorry, private community admins, this chapter does not apply — we will chat about you soon). I love and get excited when I see forums rank high for any topic. It gives me joy when people say forums are dying, and yet they still persist. For those of you who may not be familiar with SEO, as noted earlier, these three letters stand for search engine optimization. The concept is that you "optimize" a website, as best as you can, to ensure the best ranking in search engines, such as Google or Bing, who come to crawl your public content.

Some people have "expertise in SEO," and it's their profession to help online properties achieve SEO paradise of great rankings in search engines. However, they usually approach forums in the wrong way. I don't want to downplay their work, as there *are* ways they can help you, but some of their ideas are a waste of time and actually can hurt your rankings. I know it can be tough to work with them if you have no SEO expertise. Who are you to argue with their ideas? Especially if they are making suggestions on things you need to be worried about. I write the next bit for enterprise community platform vendors everywhere: Please don't be bullied by the SEO expert working for the company. You are the community expert. Community is about connections, relationships, and real human content. Not content for robots. You know the right thing to do. I hope this chapter will help you level up your SEO knowledge and to determine where the SEO person can help you.

Let me also be clear again. I don't blame SEO experts. They look at community platforms with expectations they hold dearly from working on websites and blogs. This is not how forums work. In many cases, their ideas, while well-meaning, are not appropriate for a forum at scale. For example, I regularly see requests for the ability to rewrite meta tag titles of a post, so the title shown in search engines is different from the actual title on the page. How would that work for a forum with 1,000 posts a day? No one has time to manually update titles. This is why most forum software will auto-generate meta tags from the post title. A good community manager will just change the title of a forum post if it's not clear — occasionally. There is no mass review of meta titles changed to differ from the front end. We should also never encourage wholesale title change for SEO. Community content should be in your customers' language, not how you want them to speak. We only want intervene when it's unclear. The scale and volume of most forum conversations just don't lend to worrying about such minutiae to have the proper marketing copy for robots. When a community is humming, there will be a fantastic amount of user-generated content (UGC) — too much for any community manager to review.

This is not to say the SEO experts — and you — have no SEO work to do. There is plenty to do, actually. The following advice is mainly aimed at those on hosted forums, but don't worry if you are self-hosted. These concepts are universal.

So let me start by helping you break down some of the major SEO experts' concerns, what you need to know, and where their focus can be to assist you.

URL Structure
Many SEO experts get concerned with folder depth. I won't say it's not important. You should not have folders for folder's sake. A folder in URL speak is where you see a "/" separating the elements in the URL found in the browser

address bar. However, most platforms only create folders for what is necessary for the software to work. The main thing to work on is to ensure those category names make the most sense and are relevant to the content. Don't use obscure terms or alphanumeric terms if not applicable. The category name is likely to be placed in the URL, so it's important it gets some strategic thought.

Category Descriptions

Here is something important to consider. Your forum software will likely take the description of a category for the meta description for SEO purposes. Give thought to ensure the category description makes sense for humans to read and understand on the front end, but it is also appealing for those finding it in search. An SEO expert could be handy to consult here.

Discussion Titles/Meta Tags

This is another common request, which I see a lot. I just wrote about this above. As an idea, it makes sense for a blog, where you can have two to three articles a day. It's easy to manage. What happens when a forum has thousands of posts a day? This kind of feature does not scale.

Because a forum is created by users, the titles are created by your audience. It's in the language of your audience and honestly does better for SEO, because it's *not* marketing speak. It's how your audience will likely search for that question. So as long as the title is not "Help!", you should really take a second breath before modifying the title. However, this does not absolve the community manager from cleaning up a title if it's genuinely unclear. You should use a light touch on editing titles; however, it's also where you can have the best impact on SEO. The title of discussion in a forum is the headline in the search engine results. That's why getting the title right is so darn vital.

The other thing they may ask about is modifying meta tags. Meta tags are snippets of code invisible on the public page that, for example, have a way to tell search engines a description of the content. You will typically see this under a search result explaining what the content is. However, this is a forum; this is not a blog. I am not aware of any forum platform allowing such modification, and if they are, it does not make sense or scale. You are using the wrong tool for your objectives. If you genuinely want to have an impact, reword the first couple of sentences of the post, which some forum software will automatically use for the meta tag description. Make sure, if it's a significant change, you note it was done by the community team for clarity.

In short, don't be bullied by the SEO expert approaching forums with the wrong mindset, and focus on the title the community audience sees. It needs to be as clear to the community audience what the topic is, as it needs to be for those finding it with search engines. No trickery is required.

Subdomain Versus Folder
This will be an argument I am sure will never end. For those unaware, a subdomain means your forum will be located at *forum*.website.com vs. in a folder location where it will be located at website.com/*forum*.

Google has said they treat them the same. SEO people have done some tests to show there may be an edge to folder over subdomains. Nothing conclusive, though. One or two website examples do not make it a certainty.

As someone who spent many years at a SaaS company, this comes up a lot. For all of us SaaS companies, I will say, "In a perfect world, we wish we could allow people to choose a folder or subdomain with ease. This is not the case with a hosted solution." Work with any SaaS solution, and you will see the product located at a subdomain — this is just a reality. Look at Unbounce, HubSpot, Salesforce, Marketo, WordPress VIP — all of their customer-facing CMS content is on a subdomain. Now I am not saying it's impossible, but it has a high potential for instability issues and enabling reverse proxies can be costly...all for the most minimal SEO benefit. Focus on something else that has a more significant impact. Obviously, self-hosting is not an issue, but only you and your company can decide if that is worth all the extra work.

Redirects/Archiving

Let's talk 301. A 301 redirect is a server code a page will send to tell a crawler or browser when a page is permanently moved. If a web page serves this code, a visitor will be redirected to the new page. If you have ever visited a website and went to one link, and after a second, you ended up on another page, it was likely a 301 redirect.

Now, what happens in a forum when you change a title, which usually impacts the URL (or "slug," as some call it). If you have a post in a forum, and you change the title, it's fine. In most forum software, underneath the words are usually a discussion ID. This ID remains no matter what the title is. So, it's not a traditional 301 redirect. The text in the URL changes, but the location does not change. The forum platform has your back.

However, this one-off change is not the most common request I've seen. Usually, it's a request to redirect hundreds of discussions to a root category or one page, rather than showing a proper "404 error" by removing a post. That's another fun server code to know — 404. It tells the search engine the page is gone, and there is no replacement. Now, if the content *does* have a replacement, you should set up a 301, but it should always be a one-to-one relationship. Never ever hundreds of pages to one.

Sometimes, we also get asked to add a meta tag "noindex/nofollow" to a considerable chunk of community content for "SEO purposes." Why? To somehow sculpt the SEO.

The main challenge here is that some people never realize how popular their old content is until it's gone. They did not review their analytics with a careful eye, and then they see a massive website traffic decline. The best strategy is that of curation. Move the old content to a different category, close it for discussions, and add a message that it's outdated content. As an extra step, you can also move the content to a category not "viewable" to guests, which is how search engines will crawl the content on your site. They only crawl what is public. Also, by doing things this way, you allow all the "corporate knowledge" to still exist, if ever it needs to be consulted.

If you feel the content is outdated and no longer relevant, you could add a meta tag of noindex/nofollow at the category level — but tread carefully. I've seen my fair share of mishaps from people thinking content was no longer useful, and once removed, it was near impossible to get back all the benefits it brought.

In most cases, for the one-off post, the best solution is to go to the original discussion, update the title, and add an explanation that this is more recent info. Don't delete, don't noindex; simply edit and save.

Now I must add a caveat. The above are my views on forum SEO and the requests we have gotten. There are plenty of SEO people who will agree or disagree, but SEO is much more art than science. The one question you should always ask someone requesting massive changes to your forum is, "What is the predicted SEO benefit?" The best SEO people will prioritize the nice-to-have and the must-have. Any honest SEO person will tell you that the content is critical. That is, the "richness" or depth of content, or in other words, long-form written posts with details. Extra bonus points for videos, images, or diagrams. Great content is the main foundation for any SEO success with your forum. Anything else is minor and will not have a substantial impact.

With the content being so important, where can you, the community builder, help? Glad you asked. Here is my no-BS list of where community people can have a dramatic impact on their forum SEO:

- Make sure to clean up titles, when necessary. Use "human speak" for clarity.
- Learn how to do keyword research and look at Google Trends to create relevant content (more on this ahead, I promise).
- Make sure the category names, slugs, and descriptions are descriptive, but not spammy — focus on relevance.
- Review the announced discussions regularly, so pinned topics don't take up valuable slots on the recent discussion list. Search engines start at the top of the page, so the content at the top is the most important.
- When you post content to the community, try to add a relevant image and "alt tag" (description of what the image is). Not all forum software may have that ability, but it can give you a nice boost.
- Add relevant and timely content to the sidebar, and change it frequently, so there is always fresh content.

- Make sure you have a site map. These are necessary due to the tree structure of forums. Many search engines still like site maps for content-deep discovery.
- Gain some basic understanding of Google Analytics, so you can understand community behaviour and see topics/areas of interest.

This is not an exhaustive list but should get you going in the right direction. I would also get familiar with Google Search Console or Bing Webmaster tools, which will give you insights into how search engines see your community. This will let you see how people find your community and what they search for to arrive there. It will also alert you to any problems you can bring to your SEO person for review. This is not a requirement for your success, but I always love to see this data. If this is not your bag, don't worry.

A community person has lots on their plate, so, if nothing else, your most significant SEO impact will be on the actual content — either programming such content or creating a space where people are encouraged to share. Creating this content will make your SEO efforts simpler. With content being so essential, don't worry, this is not the last we will speak about the wonderful world of content and programming! However, for those of you with non-public/private communities, we need to address what happens when SEO cannot be your main driver. If this doesn't apply to you, you can skip the next chapter — and go right to content and programming!

Chapter 16: The Private Party

I have spent most of this book explaining how to manage a mostly open community, which may have private areas. However, I have yet to speak about those communities which are entirely, or substantially, private. While most of what I have written about in these pages applies regardless, I wanted to share some specific knowledge and things to consider when managing a private community.

What Is a Private Community?

Before we begin, I want to make sure we are on the same page by defining what a private community is. This way, you'll know exactly what I will be talking about in this chapter. A private community is when there is a restriction of community content to only those on the inside. However, there are different levels to private communities. Here are the three most common:

- A community where there is limited content available to anyone who registers. The main content is limited to customers or subscribers.
- A community where a minimal part of the content is viewable — like post titles — but only someone with an account can comment or access to read and participate.
- A community locked down to only authorized customers who have a login.

Indeed, many communities will have some private areas, but this is not the type of community I will be covering in this chapter. Specifically, I want to dive into the communities where the *majority* of the content is not viewable by guests or non-customers, and, therefore, will not benefit from an SEO boost.

Why Is It Private?

This is the most important thing to understand, especially if you are coming into a new community. Why have they decided to restrict access to content? Are there security, intellectual property, or privacy concerns? Did someone not know how to use the platform and realize you could have open and closed areas? Are you in a highly competitive space where privacy is the norm (and there are no other public spaces to have these conversations)?

It's essential to have a handle on this before making any decisions. You have the opportunity with fresh eyes to see if a decision made earlier still rings true.

When Should We Be Private (and When Should We Not Be)?

There are many reasons (and industries) where it makes sense to have a partial or totally private community. I also understand not wanting to give your competitors open access to people talking about your flaws or any intel about your company. However, I think you miss a massive opportunity for discovery by not having some categories open for people to see. Remember, if you block access to everyone, you also stop Google and other search engines from crawling your site. Yes, that's right, if a guest can't see your content, neither can Google. I understand if you want to let the space be only accessible to customers to comment, but does that mean all content needs to be hidden?

Of course, this is not to say having a wide-open door works for all communities. However, many communities would benefit from an industry content category discoverable by the public. For example, imagine if you work at a bank, and you create a private community for small business customers to discuss your products. By all means, keep it private — you should — because maybe you don't want competitor banks to have an easy time competing with you. However, why not have a public space for these business owners to talk about common non-bank-related topics? It's likely customers will be seeking out small business information anyway. Why shouldn't it be in your community?

It's important to realize that the choice of private or not is not binary. Your community does not need to choose to be totally open or closed to the world. Your community can have spaces — and levels of access — and any quality community platform should be able to do this.

Whatever you decide, please spend time determining your strategy on how you handle the public areas if you have a primarily closed or private community. Don't just decide to have an open category and call it a day. If your open community space has little activity, or looks uninviting, just keep your whole community private. If you do want to create an open space, let's say for pre-sales questions, wait until that area has enough content and value before making it visible. Doing a mediocre job can actually hurt your objectives.

I've seen firsthand what happens when the public area is a poor experience. I'll share just one story of how changes to this experience can have a significant impact. One day, I was asked to join a customer call by a customer success manager. I didn't have much time to prepare, because it was so last minute. I went to their community about 15 minutes before the call. It was a sparse community. There were 20 conversations, all by the community manager, and no comments. There was lots of white space, and honestly, it looked abandoned. I thought the call would be about helping them get more members or how to encourage their community to talk more. However, having this initial experience, it was obvious no one would ever bother with this community.

When I got on the call, they asked me what I thought about their community and how they could get more customer activations. I was quite candid and said, "I would never bother to sign in as a customer. It's not compelling enough."

They sat in shocked silence. They were confused and asked if they could share their screen with me — and what they showed me was this beautiful community. I was wowed.

"Was this the same community space I was looking at?" I asked, reading the URL aloud.

They nodded. I then asked to show them my screen. I guess they hadn't really looked at the guest experience. Now they sat silent again. We then had a great conversation, and they took action. So, what did they do? They made the community 100% private, but they created a video and a landing page showcasing all the wonderful things available to customers once inside. They made sure the link was prominent on the website, and they sent an email blast to their customer list. Now, with a more explicit message around value, they saw a massive increase in customers activating their community access. In this case, staying private was the solution, but they needed to ensure the customers knew what they were getting.

I see another mistake when it comes to mixing private and public spaces. New community builders think they have a solution to solve for SEO but still keep things private. They decide to make discussions public and comments private — i.e., people must log in to see the answers. Do you know what the outcome is most times? Frustration. This is especially true when they use this tactic in a B2B support community. The person will create a throwaway account, see the comment, and never return. Why? The comment is low value and doesn't solve the problem. Or they keep searching online until they find a space that has the answer they need.

That's not to say this "hiding the answer" strategy doesn't work — but you better have compelling reasons or value for them to return. Don't rely on the gimmick to create an account to read. You'll get excellent stats of new account creation and low content engagement long term.

As you can tell, I am a fan of the hybrid community with both private and public spaces. Organic search engine discovery of your community accounts for a majority of communities. This is why I ask you to not underestimate the value of SEO to your community's success. It can help new people find you and help your customers recall that you're there. There is also a simple test to see which way you should go with this too. Take your top three or five community questions. See what comes up in Google or Bing. If there are other forums, competitors, or other spaces a potential customer can get into without logging in, you need to rethink your strategy.

If you are trying to think about how to have effective mixed private and public spaces for customers — one solution is an industry-specific space. This is an area "sponsored" by your brand, but you still have private areas for your customers to converse and share around your products. It does require lots of work, and I wouldn't suggest you try to build both at once. I am a fan of starting industry first and then the private product areas. However, I certainly understand why companies want the immediate return on investment by creating a community for customers.

I should reiterate, as much as I want to push you to consider opening an area of the community to the public, numerous private-only communities do well. They have a dedicated customer base or focus on topics that require discretion due to sensitivity or security. You may be working at one of those — and it's fine. All I ask for your customers is, if your community needs to be private, please use SSO, so we can access it easily without a separate login. Oh, and please don't hide it. Make it findable within your app or the website in your client area. Don't make it a scavenger hunt. You need to reduce friction as much as possible and remind your customers to use your community. Your internal allies in the customer success and support team will be crucial in reminding them.

What Is the Value You Are Offering (and Should They Pay)?

I recall once working with a company that was creating a paid community from scratch. They weren't famous or offering unique content. They planned from day one to charge for access to the community. To this day, I am still not clear why they thought anyone would pay. They spent so much time making the community pretty, they never made it worth the time of anyone to be there.

Let me be clear again, I am not opposed to the paid or closed community — but make it valuable. Make it part of a total offering. Give me a special unique access or offer. Let me in for a trial to see the value. Spend the time on substance. Don't make me stand behind a velvet rope to get into an empty club. I'll never come back, and I'm telling all my friends. Please don't be these people.

Actually, as I sit here, I find it hard to think of any example where paying solely for community access has worked. Usually, it has been part of a total package. Not saying it can't happen, but these examples are scarce.

The best value you can give your customers in a private community is for them to find the value quickly, with or from your product or service, self-educate, learn, connect with others (network), and accelerate their professional development. You focus on this, and you have a winner.

How to Hit Objectives (or What Should They Be)?

Generally, if your community is closed to the public, it will be because it will be customer-focused. In an open community, your goals will be more tied to marketing objectives (filling the funnel) and customer success/support. In a closed community, things are more inward. It's about education, customer value realization, reducing churn, and increasing advocacy (referable) customers. Your allies are less the marketing organization and the customer success team.

Your source of new members will be from new customers. Why? Customers will not randomly come across the community by some search. Therefore, the community should be part of customer onboarding. It will also be an essential offering to your customer success team. If integrated into their workflows, the community can help customers get deeper into the product faster and build connections.

It's also an excellent space for customer feedback (as long as you close the loop), product ideas, and support. You want to be plugged into the concepts of the customer life cycle and less on the buyer journey. In my experience, closed communities usually have some of the best in-depth content, and metrics are about the consumption of content (time on site, pages per visit, reactions per piece).

This last bit is really important to dwell on just a bit further. Don't set goals and outcomes for a private community about user growth — but on customer activation. Also, measure how people consume the content and how they feel about it (i.e., measure how valuable they find it). Reactions, surveys, and basic analytics reports should help with that.

What Else Should I Know?

Caution, my new community builder friend, on this private vs. public discussion. The main advice I want to share when launching from scratch — try to be a public community from the start. It's easier to move things private later than to worry or try to identify what private content may go public especially if there's a chance if you could open it up later.

I should add, don't feel this is something you need to tackle on day one. It's something to keep in your mind as you look at the goals and outcomes of the community. You'll want to balance the importance of discretion and other company objectives. Only make adjustments once you understand the community, your audience, and the company goals to best align the outcomes for everyone!

Chapter 17: Community Content Programming

In an earlier chapter, I covered the importance of SEO and content. Now the rubber hits the road of making it happen. How does one organize, create, and program the content that matters for a community? Don't worry, friend, this chapter is for you!

Before we get going, I want to place an image in your head. As a community manager, you are like a director of a movie. You set the direction, you may write the script (content), like some of those great directors do, or you may work closely with a writer (moderators and super users), so the vision of the story is achieved. You need to motivate the actors (your community members) to give their best performances by using your skills. You try to create a masterpiece while also keeping the studio (your bosses) happy. The goal is a box office smash that has artistic integrity, under budget, and on time. No sweat, right?

So, where to begin? This thing we keep talking about . . . content. This is a crucial element to your success. Just like on a blog, content is what the people will come for. However, in the role of community, this takes on a different tactic. Also, to be honest, the beginning of any content programming efforts may involve you simply rolling up your sleeves and creating/collaborating with others to develop this content. In some communities, this is a continuous process that never ends. Content will be part of your role, as community professional, it just varies in terms depending on the maturity of your community and the size or budget or your team. In some of the larger communities, there is a   dedicated community content person.

Creating a content program might seem like second nature for some of especially if you have content marketing experience. Nonetheless, there is a bit of a different tack here, because you have direct access to your audience. Community is a people-first initiative. In your planning, you will have met some great people, who also told you about their pains, goals, and feelings toward the concept of your community. These are the people you are creating for, and there is nothing wrong with having a small group of trusted early members to talk to about content or to collaborate with you. I actively encourage it.

Going back to our movie analogy, no movie ever goes from a finished product to the theatre without a test screening. You'd be amazed how many masterpieces were changed for the better because of audience feedback. There are also some other ways to come up with new content consistently as well. We certainly talked about content at launch, but what can you do on a continual basis?

It starts with creating a massive list of possible content at least one quarter (or more) ahead. Don't worry about production or a schedule at this moment. However, you will want to get into the habit of having content-planning sessions — including your team or people with creative ideas that intersect with your target audience. Notice I did not say "community." This is because your company audience may extend beyond your community as it is today. I like to think of the "audience" as people yet-to-be community members (but it *can* also include current community members). This is a great time to leverage your allies, such as support teams and customer success organizations. They are a wealth of customer questions, issues, ideas, and problems.

For now, though, the goal of these planning sessions will be to just write down as many ideas as you can. Invite your allies to a content session. Here is how I like to run mine for the most productive use of time. Do some work before the session and create some guidelines. Below is a typical email I may send to the allies about it:

Hi, Everyone,

As you know, we have this great community, where our customers, fans, and our audience visit to talk about our product. Creating great content for them to discuss and engage with is really important for our company to succeed with our community and to serve them better. Successful communities have more engaged customers, leading to tangible benefits for our company, like higher NPS® scores, larger order sizes, and more loyal customers, willing to leave us positive reviews on third-party sites.

You and your department have deep interactions with our customers, and I feel you may have some great insights. I would like to invite you, or any members of your team who you think can contribute, to a brainstorming session of issues, topic ideas, or problems, for which we could create content that would help. You may also circulate this email to the team, and if they want, they can send me ideas, but I prefer a planning session, so we can benefit from inspiring one another.

Below are some times I was thinking of holding the sessions, based on our availability.

- *Monday at 10:30 AM*
- *Tuesday at 3:00 PM*
- *Thursday at 5:00 PM*

Look forward to our session — and let me know if you have questions before we meet.

Now a quick word about the marketing team. Please include the marketing team — they really are an ally. I know some community managers would rather not include them, but you may want to for several reasons. They likely have some very creative ways to deliver content. They may already be working on content that may have value for the community. Another great thing? They likely have a budget to help you. I am not saying you need to 100% include them in the planning sessions, but I would ensure they are in the loop and give them an optional invite, with a promise to connect with them afterwards on the ideas that bubble up.

While content creation seems like it's not part of community-building initially, you'll come to learn it's a core part of the job — especially if you are a team of one. It's almost a given that you will create discussions at some point, but it will also include curating community content for e-books or hosting AMAs with industry experts. Depending on your role and organizational investment in community, you might simply be coordinating the content, or you may be the one creating it directly or encouraging others to do so. The intersection of content and community falls into your sphere of influence, and you should lead the charge when possible. Don't be afraid to jump! I always loved to be part of content creation, even if I did not create it myself. No matter what, I try my best to ensure any content adds-value to the community and the conversation — you can play that role too.

Planning sessions can be fruitful, especially if you are new to the business. I would also begin your time with the group by giving some brief simple guidelines. Make people feel welcome, and give them a chance to introduce themselves to the rest of the group. Make sure everyone knows that no ideas or content suggestions are stupid. Remember, this is a conversation on topics, issues, concerns, and problems, we can create content around to help our community. Keep it clear that you plan to stay on that task.

Use Post-it notes, cue cards, whiteboards or spreadsheets to capture all the ideas. Whatever works for you in the planning session. This is about getting an initial base for the quarter ahead. Indeed, you should be open to hearing ideas as they come in too. Add them to whatever format you keep them in: Google docs, forms, emails, tickets, or a section on your community. I know one person who uses a private GitHub repository. Use the tool that works best for your situation.

Hopefully, you will have so many ideas that you will cry with happiness (and maybe have a bit of fear). This is normal. On the flip side, what happens if you can't get a group together or you don't get lots of content ideas? It comes down to research. Thankfully, there is lot you can do on your own. Here's a non-exhaustive list to help:

- What are the searches people make on your community platform?
- What does your analytics tell you about website searches?
- What alternative search queries do the search engines offer?
- What are the questions your sales team gets frequently?
- What kind of content is being created by competitors or adjacent companies in their communities?

Let me also be 100 percent clear, as it may have been missed: you should also be regularly talking to the community. Survey them on the things they need, talk to your top members on a regular video call, and don't be shy about having an area in the community for suggestions on content. Imposing your view all the time regarding what issues matter for a community is a sure way to ensure the community will not engage in your discussions.

Okay, so on to this big list of things to do. What's next? Well, start writing the content, of course. Put the book down — you don't have time to read! Good luck!

Wait. Stop. Please don't do it all yourself! Remember that not all the content has to be written, and certainly not only by you. The point of the information-gathering sessions is to uncover the issues, topics, concerns, and problems the community has. The content programming in the community is how we turn these identified issues into something helpful, and it may not even need to be in written form. It should not be about the *format* of the content right now, or the delivery mechanism. The meeting should be for ideas only. Once you have the ideas, you can start talking about delivery.

Delivery is where you get to be creative — and it's my favourite part. To help you get inspire, the following subheading will share some ways to create programming from ideas that may have surfaced from your brainstorming sessions.

Ask the Experts Series
As the title suggests, find experts within the community or invite them to a conversation about key topics. When I was running a cryptocurrency community, I had the community ask their tax questions, and then I had leading tax professionals answer the questions I gathered.

In return for their answers, these tax people got exposure, new clients, and they learned what mattered most for those in the space. It became an annual tradition for the community and one of the most popular content programs I had.

Sometimes, short "experts show you the secrets" videos are compelling. Nothing overproduced is needed. This is not Hollywood, and you don't need the marketing team to over-produce it. Indeed, it's nice if they can, but really, there are only a couple of primary elements you need: be able to hear the speaker clearly and see the video easily (making sure it's well-lit). The popularity of video can take on a life of its own. I did a video for my stamp-collecting community on a microscope I bought, and it has been viewed, as of this writing, over 20,000 times. That's just insane to me. It all came from a community question too.

I know this may not apply to *all* communities. I learned a long time ago to try my best to avoid using universal indefinite pronouns; however, there is likely an angle of expertise in your community. Especially if it is in the B2B space, tap into it for a regular series.

Behind-the-Scenes Q&A with Staff

Access behind-the-scenes is almost always fascinating. What are the design philosophies of a software company in their decision-making? What are the processes from idea to implementation? How is the company structured? How do you measure success? What are lessons you've learned and advice you'd pass on? What are your favourite features, and what is the story behind them?

I know I am enraptured when Magic: The Gathering tells the stories behind the cards or when I hear the design decisions they considered and why certain choices were made. I know selling B2B can sometimes be less sexy for some, but if you are using a product in your daily life, having stories behind the product choices can be helpful or compelling. Let's not fear showing how the hot dog is made. A community appreciates the details.

197

Share Experiences/Tips Series

This is great for scenarios where you have a specific product with a long learning curve and a conservative company that does not want to be as transparent about internal processes. You create cohorts around experience and invite "the experienced" to share their knowledge and take questions on a regular occasion. Maybe once a month or in the format of "Your top 3 questions answered." You can also create "I want your feedback," "Share what you are working on," or "What I wish I knew" series in the community. There are lots of ways to get creative with this.

Package Content for Your Community into an E-book

This has always been a favourite of mine. In my earlier example regarding the expert series for taxes and cryptocurrency, we created an e-book each year with the most essential and up-to-date information. Our community had over 50,000 members, and we had almost that many downloads. I looked, and not every download was a community member, but they all learned about our community from it. Now I wasn't into it for the leads, but I can assure you, if your company is selling something, your marketing boss would love to have those leads.

Content that comes directly from the community is usually the most powerful, because it speaks to their needs. It's also why many inventions are born from people solving their own problems. I'm reminded of Bette Nesmith Graham. She invented the first correction fluid in her kitchen. But why? She was working as a typist at the time, and she sought an easier way to fix her mistakes. It became huge, and she became rich in her own right, even before her son became famous as one of The Monkees.

You can apply that lesson too. Look to the community for the problems they have and collectively "invent" a guide that makes things easier. Another way to encourage members to share their advice with the community is to ensure people who submit content get a copy of the final product before anyone else. Or maybe, if it's an e-book, you send them a physical copy with a thank you note! No better thank you than opting for the wow, if you can!

Shared Scrapbook

This is a fun project. The idea is that you start a scrapbook, where every community member has a page to design as they see fit, before passing it along to the next person via mail. At the end of a set period, the book is sent back to you, and then you make a digitized copy for everyone to have one.

This may not work for every business, if it's not a fit for their product or community. Another way to do this is to change the format. Bring this to live-action and digital, by coordinating a collaborative video. Everyone records a short video with a tip, and then you stitch it together and share it with everyone in the community.

There are many ways to tap into the collective hive mind of the community and bring them together.

Local Meetups

I've watched in admiration as the team at CMX Bevy turned a yearly event into local community-run chapters. As of this writing, they hold dozens of mini-events monthly, around community management topics, in most major cities worldwide.

Depending on the size and scope of your business, this could be something compelling in supporting your overall community initiatives. Your company may be the sponsor, and your job is between supporting these local communities and the corporate community.

Weekly Office Hours

This is a popular concept you can adapt for the community. You set aside time for a regularly scheduled hour-long video chat or space set up for community members to come and ask their questions. It could be open, or you can set up 15-minute private sessions for your shy members to sign up for. Calendly and Doodle are time-saving tools for finding mutually beneficial time slots, but use whatever method works best for you and your community.

Creators Programs

This idea comes from the gaming world, but can work in B2B, primarily if you sell a product. This is where the community helps create content, KB articles, how-to content, or videos. In return, they get a free or discounted license to your product. Other perks are beta or early access to new products. You will want to check with the legal team on these kinds of "freebies," but it can be a great way to scale up (and reward) content creators.

Phew! Quite the list, but certainly not endless. I hope it got some ideas going in your head, along with how you'll apply them to your own community. Also, don't forget you can mix it up with seasonal/holiday programming to make it even more relevant.

I know you may be raring to go create all these beautiful pieces of content, but let's take a moment to look at structure. We should also consider proper segmentation too. Not all content is for all audiences. There is no shortcut to planning, so please take the time for it. What I have found helpful is using Monday.com, but use whatever tool works for you. Whatever you choose, you should track the following:

- **Program/Content:** This is content you are creating, including the media (video, written, infographic, etc.).
- **Persona:** Which segment of your community is this content for? Newbies, experts, everyone?
- **Content Reason:** Why are you creating content, and what outcomes do you expect? Do you expect them to share, interact with comments, or create more related discussions?
- **Metric Tracked:** This should be a specific metric that is a number and measurable to define the success of the content. It can be whatever you want, but it should be meaningfully measurable. For example, it could be the number of shares, if brand awareness is your goal.
- **Resources Needed:** What resources do you need? Budget? People? Hired talent? Electronics? Be specific about who/what is required to make this happen.
- **Channels/Promotion Tactics:** How will you get the info out there? What channels? What methods? Will it be on social media? In your community? Are you relying on marketing?
- **Frequency:** How often will this program run? Daily, weekly, monthly — or is this a one-off?
- **Owner:** Who owns the creation of the content? This does not need to be the person *making* it, so much as the one making sure it's *delivered* on time. For example, it could be you ensuring that a superstar in your community meets a deadline.

- Delivery Date: When is the expected delivery of the program? When do you aim to start it?

By having all the ideas mapped out in this way, you will be able to identify any gaps. Once you have the list together, here are some thoughts to consider:

- What segments/personas did you not create content for? Should you? Let's try to make sure every segment we care about has something that matters to them at least once a month, if not more.

- What are your regular touchpoints? Do you have any? I am a big fan of keeping things predictable and steady. The goal is that the content in the community helps your members build it into their routine. Like "New Resources Wednesday" — but then make sure you have something every Wednesday!

- Is everything dependent on one person? I know you are the community manager, but what if you don't have the bandwidth? Either you need to get help, or maybe you just need to shift delivery dates. Don't try to be a superhero. Work on those things with the most significant impact.

- Do you have time? When I ask about time, I mean have you planned far enough in advance for contingencies, changing course, or making sure you're not caught off guard by a special event? I like to plan one quarter ahead to work on things to be delivered in three months. You can do as you want, but don't give yourself the stress of stuff due as soon as you think of it. Doing Halloween content on October 29th is a stress you don't need. The benefit of building in time is that you have space to maneuver, change course, or recalibrate. I know some community folks who have adopted the two-week sprint model to help with their planning.

Finally, with all this information, you can create an organized calendar so key stakeholders can follow. You also have the fun benefit of being able to mark things as complete!

Oh, and there is one more thing I want to make sure you plan for. Work in time for reflection and review of your programs regularly. Consider creating your own quarterly business review (QBR) of your efforts, especially if this is not part of your company process. Set this in the calendar, and commit to it, so it happens.

What does the review entail? An evaluation, of course! Essentially, each piece of content in your program should be subjected to several questions, but they really fall into these two buckets:

- What were the content outcomes? This is the actual outcome from your content efforts for this specific piece of content. This is an assessment of the strategy, tactics, and metrics. What worked and what didn't? Any blockers, lessons, or surprises?
- Keep doing it? That question essentially begets three options:
  - Keep doing what you did — because goals are being met.
  - Modify slightly — because, with some change, goals *could* be met.
  - Stop — the effort did not yield the results needed, and nothing can fix it.

Be honest with your review. Involve the teams needed to give feedback. Keep it in electronic format so you can refer to it in the future. Why? All your effort becomes a handy resource of knowledge for you and your team. It's a great resource to review if the same content idea comes forward in a future session. Maybe conditions change, or you have a new way to salvage an old idea that was done too early in your community life cycle.

I know all of this seems like a lot of work. I can't hide that it is. So, you may wonder if you should even bother. The truth is, without rigorous habits of creating these kinds of processes, ideas will get lost or never get fully explored. Don't think that the regular review is not necessary. Who wants to keep doing the wrong things without the results they need?

There is also a huge benefit of all your planning and keeping it in one spot coherently. When review time comes at the end of the year, and your boss asks, "What have you done?", you'll have a very detailed list. Without such a document, I would never remember all the things I have worked on and achieved during a year. Let this be your secret weapon for those conversations.

There is also one other great benefit. You have a way to pass along the information to colleagues or people who join your team as it grows. You'll have a library of things that worked or didn't, and even ideas that might be worth revisiting with fresh minds. Your future self will thank you for putting this in place from the start and taking the time to write it down.

Chapter 18: Let's Get Engaged!

Engagement. We need more engagement. We want to increase engagement. We want to measure engagement. Let's stop the insanity of using this word. The only thing that should be engaged is your brain. Please refrain yourself, or anyone on your team, from using the term "engagement" for goals. What does engagement really mean? Ask a room full of people to write down their definition of "measuring engagement" on a piece of paper. You're sure to get several different answers. Of course, I am being a bit facetious on what engagement means — we have *some* idea. Still, the point is, it's nebulous, and it doesn't change the fact that the word engagement is the "miscellaneous" of goals. It's a marketing buzzword.

I told you in a previous chapter about the importance of content, so let's consider this definition of engagement as "having people consume content" in your community. Indeed, engagement could be about community members participating, but it can also be about them interacting and consuming content. See how this word lacks clarity? However, we now also run into another issue. How is the engagement of content measured? Page views? Let's not fall into generic terms again. Page views alone are a horrible metric. Sure, you can use that as a pulse for activity, but please go a step further. We are looking to increase page views *per session*.

Push yourself. How do increased page views per session help your business? Dig deeper. I am much more intrigued, for example, if you find that, for every 50 page views, you get a new order. Aha! Now you have something to measure, a ratio of page views to the value of purchase orders from community members. Now you have a value for page views, and you are tying it to a business outcome.

When you or your stakeholders find the word "engagement" crossing any lips, push for the *real* goal. I just spoke to a customer who was keen to measure engagement. I prodded further, and they told me their goal was to turn prospects into buyers and get their current customers to share their best ideas and connect with one another. Several great things to measure. However, you can see this did not align with my idea of consumption (I did that on purpose). Remember, if you don't define engagement, it will mean something entirely different for those outside *your* brain. Please make sure you determine what your stakeholder means when they say engagement — and get it in writing — so they don't change the definition.

There is another aspect of engagement, not related to stats, but related directly to your engagement with your community as a community builder. Now before you say, "Adrian, you're not defining something you just scolded us for," I promise I will.

Being Committed to the Community Role

When I talk about being engaged with your community, I mean a commitment to participate. I will elucidate the numerous ways you can do that in this chapter. First, however, it begins with something that could be challenging. Engagement relies on commitment. I know, if you are reading this, you have that commitment. However, like a marriage, you can only have one partner. It's you and your partner. Why do I mention this? Because I often see people managing the community for their company, but they are also the marketing manager, social media manager, or in some other role.

Look, I get it. Being a community manager, especially if you're reading this, has probably come from an accidental appointment, or the classic, being "voluntold." I've been there. In all my years, I can also tell you that I have rarely seen part-time community managers be successful. It's tough to build a community when you have a community manager on shifts, or for only X hours a day. Sure, staff and volunteers can fill gaps, but you need someone committed full time. The community needs to know who the person is. Don't have 56 community managers, each taking two hours shifts.

How can you build relationships, start to recognize the upcoming people, make sure to maintain consistency in moderation, or even show your own members that they should care, if it looks like your company doesn't?

If you're building your community part time, please consider that this is not sustainable. I know some of you already realize this, but don't try to be a superhero. I fear if you try to prove community program success as a part-timer, you never really make the community as successful as it can be. If you find yourself in this situation, you need to decide. You also need to convince the company that your freedom to work on this full time has enormous benefits and impact for them. Hopefully, this is helped by showing the contribution made so far and a plan for what full-time focus could mean. How to know when to push for that head count? When you're too busy to do your community work properly, it's time for a full-time community head count. One way to help make the case is to list the things you do and things you *could* be doing to contribute even more to company goals. Tie it to the things they care about. If you are treading water up to your chin, it's time to chat with your manager before you drown.

Also, let me save time for anyone who may wish to send me a message saying that their company manages a community part time successfully. I did not say it's not *possible* to be a part-time community manager. It's just very hard, and I've rarely seen success. I'm merely suggesting it could be much more. If you have someone who is the face in the community (i.e., you) and is supported by a team who regularly shares and communicates, you might be able to get to a point where success leads to the moment where a full-time commitment makes sense. Then you will have to decide where your heart lies and take on the role or pass it to someone else.

Assuming we now have someone dedicated and committed to the community's success, how do we increase community engagement? Hahahahah. You thought I broke my own rule, didn't you. Don't worry. I will define community engagement in this context, share how you build a sense of community, create community stickiness, and develop connections and the tactics to do that. Phew!

Some of the ideas work better for new communities, some work for smaller communities, others work for all . . . and please keep in mind, this is not an endless list, but meant to inspire you. Without further ado, here are some of my favourite tactics.

Be Available

Ask anyone who has worked with me in a community, and they will tell you I have a personal SLA (service-level agreement) for all communities I work on. You don't necessarily have to publicly announce it, but I try my best to ensure that no comment goes 24 hours without someone responding or acknowledging it. I am even more eager to engage with anyone who is not afraid to start a riveting conversation in the community. These are the behaviours you want to encourage. Also, please use words or questions that elicit a further response, and not just a tap on the "like button." Make sure your community helpers know this too. Please also realize, I am not asking you to do this alone. This should be added to your community management playbook (more on this in a future chapter).

Personalized Email

If you have 10,000 people joining your community a day, this can be hard. However, many new communities or niche communities have this kind of traffic volume, so you can take the time to review who is joining the community. If your community is connected to your CRM, and you see a VIP has joined, I recommend sending a personalized welcome message. Especially if this is someone who could be a future spotlight AMA, someone who is influential in the industry, or who has experiences that would be valuable to share with the community.

With that in mind, please make sure the email is more than just a welcome message. Be specific about what behaviours you are looking for or the action you want from them. Maybe you point them to a conversation that could use their input, ask their best advice for a new user, or even invite them to share feedback directly with you about their onboarding experience. They may be an excellent resource for ensuring your community adds value for them, especially considering we want to be surveying/talking to members regularly to ensure we meet their needs.

Community Member Files

I like to keep notes on members in the community, such as things I learn about them, their birthdays, or any expertise they may have. Some use the community notes function, some people use spreadsheets. Everyone does this differently, but just know that successful communities do it. It's not to be creepy, like a spy agency (so it should not have their email, IP address, or anything like that), but includes things that may come up in conversation — and it's more to assist in *connection*.

For example, someone says they are from Denver, so you may connect them with other members from Denver. Or someone has a tax question, and you've noted a particular member regularly answers these questions, so you may ask for their help if no one responds within 24 hours. Once again, and to stress this, the information is stuff people have shared *publicly* already, and are to be used more as a trigger for your brain, since it may be hard to remember everything about members. It may also not scale as the community gets busier, but it's a great way to start building those connections and shape behaviours you want. Please, once again, don't be creepy with the info. Think of using it the way you would at a cocktail party if you were a good host. "Oh, Jim, you're new to playing the guitar. Let me introduce you to Dave, who used to have a band and maybe can give you some tips."

You may want to also keep track of their point, or reputation, in the community, so you can identify future volunteer moderators or potential people for ambassador programs. I foresee, in the coming future, this will be much easier with AI and machine learning, and I can't wait for that day.

The Specific Mention

This goes hand in hand with the prior point. It's a great tactic to mention another member, but always be specific about why you're mentioning them and what you are hoping for them to do. Please, please, please don't overdo this. Also, depending on the person/type of community, you may want to ask their permission before mentioning them in a discussion where you think they could provide valuable insight. No one in school ever likes to be called on without knowing it's happening, so try not to do that to others, unless they are cool with it. Most people are okay with a mention, but use it sparingly unless you know they are fine with it. Why? because those mentioned may get burnt out, start ignoring when they are really needed and you may actually drive away your most helpful members. It's also a horrible experience for members to always wait on one person whose job is not to answer them. Worse, they may get into the habit of mentioning these folks rather than asking the community at large. In short, use caution, or mentioning can become habit forming in the wrong ways, and alienate the core people you need to attract (and keep) to build a successful community.

In brand-new communities, some people will constantly mention the forum admin. To handle this, I am firm, but polite, in explaining that it's unnecessary to mention the admin unless it's urgent and no one can answer. Instead, all discussions should be directed to the community, and if it makes sense for me to comment, I will jump in.

Same with topics in the community — wait before you make that mention. Hopefully, another member of the community will answer or comment on a discussion. If you pass your SLA time, either comment or use a mention to ensure someone with knowledge responds.

Feedback/Interviews — Groups and 1-to-1
Consider regular check-ins with groups or individuals for a 15-minute interview or feedback call regarding what they like, what you could do more of, or how you can help them be more successful with their goals. Some things may be

beyond your control to fix due to internal company politics or IT resource limitations, but I am sure there are also lots of other things you *can* do. Showing you care for the community is essential. For this reason, try every quarter to do 1-on-1 calls with key members. You may also wish to consider a community advisory board with a group call for top members to keep a pulse on things, and direct their energy as best needed in the community.

Believe it or not, most people *want* to help if they're passionate about a topic. They will love to be asked. Make sure you spend more time listening than telling. This doesn't mean you can't use these calls to ask for help or share what you need from them. Don't be shy about giving them some direction on assisting you with community goals and objectives.

Re-engagement

Sometimes you have a great contributor who just stops. I like to look at the activity of users regularly. If I see someone consistently participating in discussions, and then they disappear for an unusual amount of time, I will reach out to just check in. It should be out of genuine concern. A simple "Hey, we miss you" message lets them know you're there for when they're ready.

However, I would do this kind of reaching out in only really exceptional circumstances. Why? Because you will need to be prepared. Sometimes the responses may be shocking — a death in the family, loss of job, other family issues. We all go through hard times, which can derail our normal behaviours, so the best you can do is be there when they need you.

Sometimes, though, it's because they forgot about your community, or they just lost their interest. Those kind of responses — especially if they are a more regular occurrence — need your attention. Maybe the community content for the most advanced members is lacking. Perhaps you should focus on more touchpoints or regular programming they can rely on. However, it's also normal for some people to just drift away from disinterest. Only you can know the acceptable community churn number, so it's great to create a baseline of "percentage of returning members by segment" to monitor this.

Also, contacting the laggards is a tactic more for the mature communities. A new community is still finding its voice, and likely, has lots of new members joining. You are still finding your voice. I would suggest, unless your attrition rate is abnormal (e.g., 99% of members never return), you want to focus on fostering potential all-stars and continue keeping the interest of members up front. Chasing those who drop off is a matter of bandwidth rather than that of not caring. If you have the bandwidth and it makes sense, there is nothing wrong with reaching out. I know you can automate these types of emails, but I have always been a fan of the more personal outreach.

Talking to Lurkers

Ever been to a dance and had someone drag you onto the dance floor? Did you enjoy that? What if you were in the corner of a party, just taking it in, and someone yelled at you from across the way, "You should eat these delicious meatballs I made!" and now the whole room's energy is focused on you.

Don't be the community manager who makes those who choose to lurk feel uncomfortable. If they want to dance, they know where the dance floor is. If they like meatballs, they will eat them. Many in the community business are now calling lurkers by another term too — as they have value. They are, instead, calling them "learners" or "consumers" (because they consume content). I quite like that approach, because it removes the negative associations of the word lurker. These individuals are still silently learning from the community. They are your "page views without comments" people. They may be the "share on social without comment in the community" people. They may even be "problem solved, and I liked the comment because I don't need to create a ticket" people. These are not bad behaviours. You don't always have to turn lurkers into discussion starters. However, you can create a space that makes people feel welcome when it's their time to communicate and think they have something to contribute.

Lurkers are the community equivalent of teenagers who respond "okay" when you ask them how their day was. When they want to participate, they know where you are. In most communities, this number can vary from 60% to as high as 90%. I would not worry about engaging them, but I would watch their behaviour as they watch you. Ahhhh, you ask, what do I watch for? Use your analytics to segment them to watch their page views per visit, time on site, and other consumption metrics. If these stay stable, things are fine. If the cohort has a huge spike in the wrong direction, you need to investigate. Did something change? Can they still log in? Was popular content removed? Are the conversations moving into less interesting topics? This cohort is your silent majority. Time to take action.

And remember, just because they prefer consumption, doesn't mean they won't ever participate. When they are ready, and you hit the right topic, the shy will feel like joining. This is especially true if you're focused on making the space welcoming and safe.

There is something great when you embark on creating the content, but it's so much better when doing it with the assistance of the right tool. Paper maps are fine in helping you navigate, but a GPS system is so much easier. The same happens when planning, designing, and promoting content. There are many different types of software that can help you — and I want to share.

So what are these services, software, and technology you should be aware of? This was one of the hotly contested passages in my book. I have rewritten this passage a lot. If we were sitting together, we could have a good chat about it. I could come to understand what you are building and your experience level. I could make proper suggestions. I'd likely know a tool or two you could use. You might even share some with me.

Then I went down the rabbit hole of permanence of print. Does it make sense for me to recommend services or companies that may be gone in 12 months? What if new tools come out? It could also make this book not age well. I hotly debated this with myself one Friday morning at 5:17 a.m. with my cat staring at me. She and I came to the agreement that, as you read about the different types of technology, focus on what the technology allows you to do — as opposed to any specific company suggested. Also, hopefully, you are reading this at a more normal hour of the day.

One more note. This is also not an endless list. It was hard to know what to include and what to skip. How do I know what tools you know? Better to share the list of tools I use and let you decide which you can skip. So don't be shy. My main goal here is to modify your mindset that you need to do everything by hand. There are technology solutions to make life easier. Without further ado, let's jump into the technology.

Marketing Automation

If you're not aware, marketing automation is your marketing department's secret weapon. If you are a marketing manager, it's likely you know it well, and you may be confused why I have it on the list.

Well, it's because you can add your marketing automation tracking code onto the community too. What does that do? You'll be able to see how the customers are interacting with the company overall and the content within the community. This can assist in content creation or segmenting your community audience. Your team can get creative with lists around behaviour within your marketing automation tool to help you create/analyze those segments.

It also is an effective way to engage based on behaviour, so your team can send offers, touchpoints, and other content of interest, using another aspect of marketing automation...the power of workflows. Workflows are triggers you can create in your marketing automation software that fire based on the behaviours of a specific member in the community (and the rest of their digital journey).

For example, if they achieve a rank in your community, it could trigger a CRM update, send an email to a swag provider, and countless other things. It can also help *you*, business teams. For example, if Johnny is spending an inordinate amount of page views and time in a category about a new product, your team can send him an offer for a discount.

I know some pure community people will be appalled by this, but let me say, I want my readers to also keep their jobs. Having the community help achieve marketing or sales team goals is not evil. The evil happens if you let that be your driving cause at the expense of building human connections, and you forget to be building community with a people-first mindset.

I actually encourage you to look at those sales and marketing goals. As I have written about, be impactful with your goals. Work with the marketing team and control how messages come to the community. Don't be a blocker. Be a community champion and a filter, to ensure the messaging always is clear as to "what's it in for them" (in other words, value for your community members).

One final thought on automation: it's not necessarily just about *marketing* automation. Automation, in general, can make you into a superhero. This is where something happens in tool X, and it triggers something in tool Y. You can look at a tool like Zapier, which connects with over 3,000 other solutions. It can really make your life easier. I don't have the space to go through all the ways you can use it, but it's worth exploring with your ecosystem. I found integrating the online community with chat tools like Slack to be very powerful for helping with internal community adoption and awareness of community content.

Email Software

Many marketing automation solutions will likely also have some sort of email marketing capability. Early on, Mailchimp, Mad Mimi, or Constant Contact were my go-to tools as I created my community newsletters (before they had automation abilities). And then I was convinced of the errors of my ways by a boss, who pointed out that marketing automation platforms already have email as a core function.

You know what else? By using one system, I found that we avoided overlapping emails and swamping our members with too much noise. Also, there was another benefit...legal compliance.

For example, if a customer unsubscribes from receiving all emails from your company, did you know it is your responsibility to make sure their unsubscribe request is fulfilled through *all* providers you're using? If you're using more than one, who needs this headache?

I haven't even gotten into all the aspects of email hygiene, database management, and all the yucky stuff you can read elsewhere. But the fewer tools, in this case, the better.

Another reason your friends in marketing can be good allies is that they can help get your community content to your audiences. In short, having a good and close relationship with your marketing team will help your success immensely.

I feel for you if you are both the marketing *and* the community person. Short term, you can automate lots of things, but it's a lot of work, that fails without someone managing the community full time. I know firsthand. If you have a chance to do community full time, please take the chance. Your marketing skills will get plenty of use.

Social Listening

Hello, my friends, working on both community forums and social media. I applaud you. These are not the same roles. There are many complementary skills, but we agree they are not the same.

I won't pretend to have social media guru skills, and this is not a book about social communities either. However, listening to what the wider community thinks about you and your brand is really important. There are many free and low-cost tools to follow your company's brand name mentions. I encourage you to listen to what people are saying. You don't need to respond always (cause that can be creepy), and if you are at a large company, someone else will likely do that. However, sometimes it makes sense. Your company certainly has guidelines (or should), but this is not our goal now. It's to get the pulse of the wider potential community members, who can join your party, and for the things they care about. Live research in the wild. I've been a fan of BuzzSumo, Brandwatch, Talkwalker and Hootsuite for this kind of monitoring.

User Onboarding

If you read this far, I know you'll spend the time creating fantastic content to get your community forum members situated on how to use the platform of choice. However, you can do more. There are services, like Whatfix, Appcues and WalkMe, that can add a bit of interactive self-help or triggers to showcase elements of your forum and website. It's really a handy way for people to see by doing.

Alerts and Trends

Alert and trend tools are the web equivalent of social listening. Essentially, there are services that will email you if your brand or your community is mentioned out in the wild. Google offers Google Alerts, but I prefer Talkwalker Alerts because they seem more consistent and reliable.

I also like to look at Google Trends, primarily geographically, to see if things in the macro world match my internal data. It's essential to ensure you break that bubble of company optimism, to see what is happening in the larger world.

I should caution, this listening will likely fail at scale, when working at a huge B2C or consumer brand. There is probably too much noise to be effective. The same is true at a large B2B corp. Thankfully, if you are this big, you likely have a whole department doing this work. If you can, I recommend making friends with that area of the business.

It's an extra win to be kept in the loop on what people are talking about. It's good to be informed and aware of the global trends and perceptions around your brand. It can also be an excellent way to get insight into trends that could impact your community work.

Graphics

Sometimes you have an excellent idea for a quick meme or need a quick graphic — but what happens when you have no time for a designer? Or maybe there is limited budget for "community needs"? Thankfully, technology has caught on to design basic images. There are a couple of platforms like Pablo (by Buffer) and Canva, which make basic graphic design sooooo much more accessible. Drag and drop. Check. Stock photos that aren't so stocky. Check. Shape tools and proper sizes. Check. Reasonably priced for budget. Check. Downloadable. Check.

I am a big fan of images and adding visual language to your online community wherever you can. There are many learning styles, and pictures are a great way to engage those in your audience who prefer visual cues. This can be banners in your community or tiles for your categories. Use these tools and have fun getting the simple design work you need quickly and easily.

Video

As of this writing, Google tends to favour videos, especially when one searches for how-to content. This is why encouraging customers or fans to create videos that can be shared in your community is a fine idea. There are also many great video-hosting tools for your business to consider, such as Vimeo, Wistia, or Vidyard. Video is also a great way to showcase elements in the community they should be aware of.

Technology has taken leaps and bounds from when I started in marketing. Now most of us walk around with a quick way to create video (and make calls too). However you take video, you can now edit them easily with affordable tools, such as TechSmith's Camtasia or iMovie. You can really make something very professional-looking without paying crazy amounts of money. Lumen5 is a solid solution that allows you to splice up video, add words, and make an ad agency-worthy piece quickly.

In some of my past roles, I was deep into video production and video creation, but this is not something necessary for a community manager to do. However, if you have the interest and the inclination, it's nice to know the existing tools. Personally, I have found video to be the best way to help people feel like they know who you are. It's a quick shortcut to making connections.

Calendar and Planning

How do you manage what you are doing and when? Everyone has their tricks. You can run a separate calendar in Google, sure, but what about things with deliverables? I like to use light project-management tools like Trello, but recently, Monday.com has become a fave. I have friends who live and die with Asana or Basecamp. Everyone has their choice. Whatever the solution, make sure it's something that is simple enough for your needs, and that those you rely on will also be okay to use.

Notes and Records

Okay, I will admit it. I am notorious for still using a pen and paper. However, this is not always possible in some scenarios. I like to use various note apps for ideas and inspiration, and Google Keep, Evernote or Microsoft

OneNote are all great for this task. Apple Notes is my current go-to.

Spreadsheets can be workhorses, but sometimes a CRM is even better. I don't mean a sales CRM in terms of opportunities and leads. I am talking about a CRM where you note that a member may like stamp collecting and baseball, because they've mentioned it and you want to make sure to connect them with someone else who may have such an interest. This may not scale alone, but it can facilitate more thoughtful and meaningful introductions. You can use Airtable to roll your own, and there is a burgeoning space of personal CRM apps out there. Or you can just use a spreadsheet. Whatever works.

Survey

At some point, you will need (or want) to ask questions to the membership of your community. This could be a sense of community survey, what they like or hate about the community design. Maybe you want to measure an effort score. How about customer satisfaction? There are several tools at varying prices, but your decision will depend on the complexity, budget, and needs. Your company may already have these tools, so it will be easy to leverage them for your needs. At the very least, I recommend you do a community survey every two years, with smaller surveys in between. If you are not asking the community about their needs, how do you know your community is living up to its full potential and whether you're supporting them?

Considering we are talking about surveys, I will also recommend you do not do community-specific NPS ® (Net Promoter Score®). "How likely is it that you would recommend our product/service to a friend or colleague?" Have you ever seen this question? It's usually accompanied

222

by a slider, or a way to choose a score from 1 to 10. This is a Net Promoter Score ® Survey.

If a customer responds with a 9+, you are counted as a "promoter." They are considered a "detractor" if they select a number under 6. Scores of 7 or 8 are not counted, as they are known as "passives." To get the NPS® score, it's a simple formula where you subtract the percentage of detractors from the percentage of promoters. Positive scores are seen as good, and if you get scores above 50, that's exceptional!

So why am I telling you about NPS®? I was recently asked about "my suggestions" concerning asking NPS® questions in a support community, and I figured this would be as good a space as any to write about this. There are certainly many good reasons to measure NPS®. However, there are some serious drawbacks to using NPS® within an isolated context of a community experience. It could also likely lead to potentially skewed scores. So, what is someone to do? And how should it be approached?

In my experience, and in working with our customers, there are a couple of ways they approach NPS® with their community. One way, the most common, is that it's all handled by your marketing team. They run their NPS® surveys as they would, independent of actions in the community, and more globally across all digital efforts. Afterwards, they correlate the NPS® results to those respondents who may be community members. In my career, I have seen an engaged community have a direct (and positive) impact on NPS®, related to brand satisfaction and even economic impact of larger orders. However, they were not looking at the direct community interactions at the time, but how the community's most engaged members felt about the brand. If someone is coming to your support community especially, asking NPS®

questions at that moment will likely reflect their frustration and not be an appropriate or realistic measure.

If you run a support-focused community, I would consider capturing a customer effort score (CES) instead. The objective of customer effort scores is to measure the effort made by a consumer to carry out an action or a process you want to know about — in our case, the interaction with the community. A low CES score implies that a visit to the community was smooth in achieving their objective, whereas a high score would indicate a problem.

When connecting both CES and NPS®, research is on our side. The 2020 TSIA Support Services Benchmark determined that CES had a direct correlative (and positive) impact on your NPS®. The beauty of CES is that it focuses not on the feeling the visitor has on the brand, but on the customer's community experience at the time of the visit.

This is why it's crucial to ensure the trigger for the survey comes at the end of the community session. You may have noticed this on other websites you visit, usually as a pop-up with the question: "Do you agree to take a survey at the end of your visit?"

There is also another benefit of adding additional questions, especially for support communities, including uncovering the data concerning if (and how) your visitors were able to solve their problems. It's not only asking about effort — you can include some questions about satisfaction. Here are some of the questions you might consider:

- What was the purpose of your community visit today? (Give them options, like looking for information or looking to solve a problem.)
- Were you able to achieve what you wanted? (Yes or No.)
- How much effort did you have to put forward to achieve your goal? (Scale of 0 to 5.)

- How would you rate your overall experience with the community today? (Scale of 0 to 5.)
- Do you have any specific feedback that could help us improve your community experience? (Text field.)

It's a simple, quick, and powerful way to gather insights that an NPS ® survey may miss. Not only does it help with ROI calculations (for example, visits that didn't require a support ticket), but it also measures the effectiveness of the community in addressing the visitors' needs. Finally, the survey data can help make decisions to improve the community, such as in discoverability (e.g., category structure), or address issues that could arise quickly if left unchecked (e.g., missing or incomplete info). In turn, asking the community these questions (and taking action) creates an opportunity to improve customer satisfaction.

Another type of survey some communities have begun to adopt/adapt is the product-market fit (PMF) survey. The PMF survey asks the customer one very specific question: "How would you feel if you could no longer use [this product]?" They then have a several choices:

- Very disappointed
- Somewhat disappointed
- Not disappointed (which isn't useful)
- N/A (I no longer use this)

Sean Ellis, noted growth hacker, came up with the survey format, and started the popular 40 percent rule. This rule suggests if a company scored below 40 percent for very disappointed, they would struggle to reach traction with their product.

I see some in the community space now adopting this question into a "community fit" question: "How would you feel if we closed this community?" This can be a quick way to determine whether you are on the right track — by asking a follow-up questions about things to improve.

Analytics

This may be last on the list, but it's, undoubtedly, first in my heart. I spent years working on an open-source analytics project, so I am keenly interested and aware of the importance of analytics measurement. It's not about data puking or measuring vanity things like page views. However, it's about measuring the right things, providing insights, and taking action on them.

I won't focus on tools, so much as I will recommend you read and follow Avinash Kaushik. He will change the way you approach your numbers. I love Avinash's constant call to analytics practitioners to ask "So what?" when it comes to the data. If you are going to measure something, the idea is you will do something with the data. Otherwise, why bother? He has had an enormous impact on my worldview on analytics and especially in setting community goals. You should have clear business goals and present them in a concise and actionable way. Don't just send tables of data.

There are numerous tools like Matomo, Hotjar, Crazy Egg, Webtrends, and, of course, Google Analytics to consider. If your company has a digital presence, they likely have a tool. You'll want to ensure your community is measured as part of the total digital ecosystem. Ensure whatever code you need is added to the community, so you can measure impact across all your company's digital channels. If you're lucky enough to have an analytics person or department, they will likely be eager to help you. They love a good mission.

A couple of minor points as you read ahead. First, almost anything can be measured, including connecting ROI, case deflection, or more. It's a matter of proper workflows, triggers, and pixels. Any competent analytics person should be able to assist. However, please don't bog them down with measuring things that, for lack of a better term, are "empty calories." Make sure what you measure makes sense (i.e., has a business impact) and is actionable. This is the data you will report up. For other things, such as community health, just use your community platform analytics, which should have what you need.

The second point is important for people new to analytics solutions. Two analytics systems will not match perfectly. There are tons of variables involved. There can be bots, which one system may block, and another does not. There are users with extensions who may prevent specific trackers. There are also varying levels of how web browsers handle privacy and tracking out of the box. Let's not even get into the fact that analytics tools may measure sessions or users differently.

Then comes the big problem: some people take the Google Analytics number as gospel and feel any other tools must be wrong. Undoubtedly, one should start with data quality; however, if no errors are found and you're at a loss to solve the issue, focus on trends. Are *more* people commenting? Superb. This is a rising number! It doesn't really matter if the two analytics systems are not exact. The trend is positive. That's how you need to look at most numbers. Analytics are not infallible, but some folks get tricked by the precise numbers or decimals places included. For this reason, try by default to go beyond the numbers and look to the trends.

I'd like to now share a short story that demonstrates this. It was for a community I ran for very tech-savvy members. I created a script that counted people blocking my analytics trackers via an AdBlock add-on. I had a hypothesis that tech-savvy members would block analytics, and that my traffic was under-reporting based on the other activity I could see. After running it for a month, I learned half of my visitors were blocking standard trackers. So, in essence, my analytics reports were really a subset of the total audience. However, by knowing what percentage was not tracked, I could use trends in a much better way to approach the data to make decisions. So even if numbers were low for a category or a topic, I needed to look at trend lines and not just raw numbers. This was an excellent lesson in tech industries, where AdBlock may be very prevalent. Once again, don't get hung up on raw numbers — focus on the trends. Also sorry for the analytics nerd talk. You were warned that analytics were close to my heart.

Are your creative juices are flowing? I know I am pumped! But what's next? How about getting some help? Nodding your head? I've been there too. Yes, you may be a sole community manager today, but that doesn't mean you have to manage it alone. Let's learn about moderators in the next chapter!

Chapter 19: Building and Managing a Moderation Team

If you are starting your community from scratch, at some point you may become overwhelmed by the work. Or maybe you decide it'd be nice to have a weekend where you don't need to worry about the community having a major drama while you're gone. Or maybe, heaven forbid, you actually need a vacation. Community work is not life or death (in most cases), but it can be emotionally draining. When you lead with empathy, it can be exhausting, and self-care and taking time off are essential. You will need to take a break, and not burst into hives thinking about the prospect.

This is not the only reason you want help with the community. It's also because your role as a community manager should evolve as time goes on and move away from managing day-to-day and become more about governing. Think of this example. You are the mayor of your city, and despite your best efforts, there is more garbage in the park. Not large debris, but enough that the park is getting dirty, and it's a nuisance. You simply can't keep up with it. What would a mayor do? Push to hire or recruit volunteers to help manage the garbage in the park. Similarly, if your community succeeds and becomes popular, you will need reinforcements to help keep things clean.

In this chapter, I will share with you how to build and manage a great moderation team, so you can relax a bit more easily. Let's begin with the first and most important thing.

How Do I Get the Help I Need?

I won't bullshit you. Sometimes it's hard to get your company to recognize that you need help, especially as you have yet to prove yourself. However, as you build your plans focused on impact, the value your work brings makes it evident you need support. As your management comes to trust you and sees your progress, you can begin to have conversations about getting help. Only you can judge your situation.

The most successful ways I have seen people get moderation help is by pointing to one of three things: ROI, brand risk, or vacation coverage needs. However, unless you have a company thoroughly invested in community success, you will likely need to rely on a combination of volunteers or staff "helping" you cover the community. I don't want to sugar coat things — this scenario is most likely. Please don't be too discouraged though, especially if you don't get help right away. If you execute well and have patience, I believe you can make a strong case for moderators — especially when you can show impact on the work you do. This is why I am so adamant that we measure what we do and how it impacts the important stakeholders, so you can show what you could do with more.

In the meantime, especially if you have "part-timers," the community playbook information shared below will be crucial so you can take off the time you deserve.

What Are Moderators, Do I Need Them, and How Many Should I Have?

Let's start by telling you what a moderator does. I mean, isn't it hard to fill a role if you're unsure what a moderator actually does? So, what exactly is a moderator, and how does a moderator differ from a community manager?

Moderators have a crucial role once you grow to the point you cannot do it alone, or when you should be moving into the more strategic role of managing the community experience.

In the simplest terms, a moderator helps you enforce the community's guidelines. They can be volunteers, staff, or a professional service (more on this in a moment).

What are some of the tasks a moderator might do? Well, it depends on your needs, but here are some example tasks you could ask them to participate in:

- Removing content
- Keeping discussions on topic
- Rewriting titles for clarity/SEO
- Curating content
- Splitting and merging topics
- Applying and helping adapt guidelines
- Much, much more . . .

They may also have only partial moderation responsibilities, such as only in subsections of the community or only for specific languages — it all depends on organizational needs.

Before we get deeper into building the moderation team and learning more, please take heed that there is no one-size-fits-all solution. Every community needs to have a conversation about moderation at some point. It usually starts when you grow beyond a certain point of activity when someone (and not you) needs to be available while your sleep or take vacation to monitor and manage the community. When the time comes, you will need to answer these questions: What happens if there is a debilitating software bug reported at 3:00 a.m. on a Monday? What if illegal content is posted while you take a sick day? Or worse, a suicide threat is posted after work hours or on the weekend?

Some companies don't have a plan, or they are willing to take the risk, to work within business hours. Only you can decide what works best for you and your company. Small B2B communities may feel they have less of a need, but as you grow, so will the importance of this conversation.

If you're now ready to have the "we need moderators" conversation, it's almost natural to hear this question: "How many moderators do I need?" Sadly *The Hitchhikers Guide to the Galaxy* by Douglas Adams got this wrong. The answer for everything in life, the universe and everything in this one instance is not likely 42.

I wish I had a magic number (like 42) to tell give you, but the truth is, no one has the right number. It doesn't exist. So how can you decide? The answer is this: You need to have enough coverage to accomplish what you need and then set your moderation levels based on those goals.

So, what do you want to do? Do you want to keep an eye on all content? Do you want the team to take action on only flagged content within four hours? Do you want them answering community questions directly, rather than letting the community respond? Once you know what you want, there are some key questions you will want to consider to help you with your head count calculations:

- How many tasks can one person handle per day?
- How much time will it take to achieve our moderation goals on a busy day?
- How many moderators would that workload represent?
- What is our company willing to spend, or capable of spending, on this (if anything)?

- Can we leverage volunteer efforts from the community itself to cover the gap on what we can't pay for?
- Do we have an international audience expecting 24/7 coverage?
- Do we see substantial activity on the weekend and after hours?

These are all questions that will help you determine how many (if any) moderators are needed.

What Is the Difference Between Moderators and Community Managers?

Before we delve deeper into moderation teams (and maybe I should have hit upon this sooner), it might be helpful to discuss the delineation between what a moderator does and the responsibilities of a community manager. Let's take a deeper look.

Community Managers

- Set policy and tone
- Drive community adoption
- Work with teams on promotion
- Decide long-term strategies
- Are the face of the community internally and externally (as needed)
- Manage the moderation team

Moderators

- Enforce the rules
- Have daily or frequent interaction with users and content
- Report up community trends and issues
- Are an important voice for the members

In summary, a community manager is an oversight position, but moderation is a day-to-day role, deep in the community's content. It's also a combination of art and skill of knowing when to jump in and when to let the community do its thing. I'd also like you to be very careful with this list. The delineation between the two is not written in stone, and each community is unique. The community manager should decide which tasks moderators handle and ensure it's clear to them as well.

What Are the Different Moderation Models?

So, we've touched a bit on this above, but essentially, there are three types of moderation sources. Let's look at each one.

Volunteer Moderators

This is probably the most cost-effective moderator, but it's also the easiest to mess up and could cause legal issues. I am not a lawyer, of course, so check with your legal team, but there is case law around for-profit companies using volunteers moderators. As some have said: "For-profit companies don't have volunteer moderators, they have plaintiffs." So do your homework about the protections you need to put in place.

If you decide to move forward with volunteer moderators, be warned, as well, that selecting volunteer moderators is hard. It takes some intuition and knowledge to assess people. You will get better, but even the best make mistakes. No community manager is perfect, and anyone giving you advice, who tells you they are, should be avoided. Self-awareness is an essential skill as a community manager. You need to know when to ask for help and where your skill set needs assistance. I know I can't be there to help you select a moderator, but I can give you the best advice I have and how I have seen it be successful.

So how do you find exemplary volunteers? Some will tell you to put out a call for volunteer moderators, but I would not do that. I prefer to use an application process, which makes it harder for the wrong kind of people to slip through. I have been a fan of identifying and offering someone the opportunity to apply, rather than putting out a cattle call.

Also, if you've been doing this for a bit, you probably already know people, or have candidates in mind, who meet certain criteria. If you don't have a list, what criteria should you consider? First off, for all things holy, never select a moderator solely based on them having lots of posts, or because they approached you to ask/beg to have the position. Be suspicious of those members. Ahhh, so you say, "Adrian, what should I look for?" Here is a non-exhaustive list of things to look for:

- People with the right temperament (e.g., consistent and positive)
- Detail-oriented in their answers (and helpful)
- Ability to communicate and write effectively
- Those who have not been shy about coming to you for clarification on rules or to point out issues with the content
- Welcoming to new members and making meaningful recommendations
- Polite and helpful (it's okay for them to tell people to use the community search to find answers, but they shouldn't be rude or abrupt in their tone)
- Community-focused, sharing helpful resources
- Those who recognize and uplift others in concrete ways for their community contributions

235

(not simply giving effusive praise without reason)

In short, choose team players who make your community a better place to be and have a sense of caring for the space. I know these people are hard to find, but there is more damage to be done by just giving anyone authority "just to help." You will rue the day.

Please also move slowly with any volunteer moderator you select, which means not giving them too much power to start. Give them training, a moderator handbook (we will delve more into this in a bit), and a quick and easy channel for them to reach you in emergencies.

Finally, what about pay? While the motivation for some volunteers is their love of the community, the topic, or the brand, tread carefully. As I mentioned before, if you are a for-profit business, unpaid moderators, especially in the US, can pose some legal risk, so please check with your legal team.

Staff Moderators

This is the most common (and safest) avenue for the majority of for-profit companies. Hopefully, you can use the concerns over brand risk and avoiding lawsuits as leverage to get paid help from your management. If you are measuring your goals and outcomes for impact, you should be able to show them why the investment will make sense. However, and this sometimes happens when you're lucky, you will get internal support from the company with little to no asking.

Depending on the situation, you may not be able to choose the people you get for the position. When this happens, training and clear guidelines will be essential. It also brings us to consider the kind of moderation goals you have. It might be that all you want to ensure is a spam-free experience during off-hours in North America. Your help is from Europe-based individuals. In a support scenario, it may be that all posts get some sort of action within a stated company internal or external SLA (service-level agreement). For example, as I shared earlier, my baseline is a response within 24 hours during the business week.

If you have a chance to select your own people or to interview staff to assist, you'll want to look for the types of criteria we seek in volunteers. I'm also a big fan of working with those people internally at your company who naturally spend time in the community.

Sometimes, actually, the community itself can be a hiring ground. You see someone doing great work in the community, and you can bring them on contract. I have seen some companies use their overseas support staff to "keep an eye" on the community for light moderation while another region is not available. Finally, another option is getting an intern from a university to assist. This is a trend I have seen become more popular in the United States in the last couple of years.

Professional Services

Thankfully, there is a third option if the other options are not possible. There are companies you can employ, such as ModSquad, Quiip, and countless others, who have already hired the proper moderators for you. They have experience with many platforms and have a process and structure to make things easier for you. They can easily (and quickly) fill whatever gaps you have in your moderation goals. They will work with you on your plan and give you peace of mind when you sleep or decide to take a vacation.

What Should I Know About Community and Moderator Guidelines?

No matter which type of moderation you decide to go with, the management of moderators is essential, and at the core, it's about human resource management, consistency, and processes.

I often see people hire or appoint a moderator and assume they will know what to do or give them very little guidance. Remember, people are not in your head. One of the reasons McDonald's was as successful as it was, and still is, relates to having very detailed guidelines for success. They strive for consistency in all locations, so if you have a Big Mac in Milwaukee or Montreal, you will recognize it as such. It is a core part of their success. Their training at Hamburger University is legendary.

Before you have a panic attack, I am not asking you to build a university, but I am suggesting that you should meet with your moderation team regularly to keep consistency. Discuss any actions taken and give them feedback/clarifications on the policy as needed (more about this later in the chapter).

Please also create private spaces to ask questions, discuss issues, and clear-up any confusion around community guidelines. Along with this space, and regular meetings to ensure your team consistently applies the community guidelines, you will need one more thing: To ensure that all your expectations are laid out in writing in a way that your team can refer to them as needed. This will become your moderator guidelines handbook. What should it include? To start, it should be a detailed and expanded version of your community guidelines. It should also cover how the community operates regarding registration, content expectations (what is allowed or not), and the moderator's responsibilities. It should include the tone the moderators should use, and finally, how to/when to/who to ask for help.

Be aware, though, that anything in your moderator guidelines should (where appropriate) have a public-facing community guideline component and be changed if it does not match. Your community needs to know the rules, and they should know what is acceptable and what is not. Don't have a set of rules that only your moderators know. Your community members need to know them too. Here is a recent example. During the early days of the coronavirus pandemic, some communities took a stance on discussions about COVID-19. However, they did not tell the community, and would just delete the content because they felt it was a B2B space. I understand, in a B2B community, where the mission is not centred on COVID-19, they might certainly make this decision. However, you break your community's trust when you delete your members' content without telling them why, or at least warning of the policy. In short, be clear and public about your content rules so you don't place your moderators in an awkward situation.

What Other Information Should Your Moderators Have?

When you ask or hire people to cover your community outside your business hours, when they cannot check in with you, they need to know how to proceed when there are issues. We can call this portion of the moderation kit a "situational playbook." It's a living document where you can add examples and modify them as needed in concert with your team. It should include everyday situations that can occur within the community (such as spamming) or serious situations requiring special care (such as someone making a threat of suicide). It usually includes suggested responses, resources, escalation procedures, and even potential email templates.

As much as I would like to give you something you can copy and paste, I can't. You need to build one, as they are unique and specific to each company, community, and geographical region. If you're lucky, maybe a friend will share their company's book with you. However, without something to copy, here are some ideas of the topics one should consider covering:

What do you do if a community member is harassing another member?

What does the platform allow for from a technology perspective? When should law enforcement be involved? What is your definition of harassment, and is it clear in the community rules? Are they warned? Banned? Are they kidding? A troll? Does this need to be escalated to the authorities?

What do you do if someone threatens suicide?

What actions will your community team take if this happens? Personally, I was fortunate to work with Patrick Groome from Penny Arcade. Their policy, which he admitted might be flawed, seemingly produced good results. If a user appeared to be undergoing some kind of meltdown or threatened to harm themselves, the moderation team would isolate the individual from the community. It was to prevent them from using the forums as a form of crisis counselling or therapy. Instead, they would provide links to suicide hotlines and other appropriate resources. He told me that, in every case where he dealt with a public threat, the user cooled down and was welcomed back with open arms. It also stuck in my head how he dealt with this, because I have never had to deal with this type of situation. At its essence, the core message was clear: It was not that people don't show support or compassion to members who may be having a rough time in their life; it's that there are limits to what untrained people in your community can do to help people in crisis. I hope you never have to deal with this situation, but I suggest you think about how you would deal with it *before* it happens.

What is the process if a member of the community dies?

This may depend on the person, but something to consider is how you want to handle their account — if at all — or memorialize them. How do you determine if they are, in fact, deceased? I know it's a tricky question to ask, but you want to make sure the info is legitimate. If the account is sensitive or high profile, it should be locked until public verification by a newspaper obituary.

What is the process if a member "rage quits"?

For those that don't know, a rage quit is when someone suddenly freaks out and, at worst, wants all their content removed in a very forceful and immediate way. Essentially, they decide to take their ball and go home. In general, I am not a fan of deleting content, especially for the all the holes it can create in a conversation. I always try to get to the root cause. Maybe they need a name change. Perhaps they need a time out. You are not a therapist to work out their issues with them, but it's good to have a policy. For example, you may have a 48-hour hold period on the request to ensure they still feel the same way about having their account truly deleted once they've calmed down.

What is the process for deleting a member's content?

See above for my concerns about deleting content. However, don't be an asshole either and dig deeper. Did they post something under their real name that could get them fired? Are they only asking about one post with no comments? Sometimes, a simple solution is changing their username or editing it (with a moderation note), so the essence of the content remains.

What if a "good" member posts spam or promotional content?

Will they be treated the same way as a bot and be banned immediately? Will they receive a warning? Who decides? What are examples of the messaging/email you expect your moderation team to send?

Why would your team need to moderate the content of a member?

So, rather than "how to edit content," which you may cover in the moderator guidelines (e.g., make a note on the post that it has been moderated by the team), your playbook would list examples of *why* your moderation team could, or should, make a change. Maybe it's because it has only the word "help" in the subject line. But what if the member posts personally identifiable information (PII) by accident — what is the process? For example, what if they accidentally post their credit card number or passport info in an image? How is it handled? Who is notified?

What do you do when it's all on fire?

What is the process if someone thinks the community has been hacked or your main website is down? Who is called? Who is responsible for the communication? Where can the moderators get info needed to update the community? What is the location of status updates?

Your playbook should include when to involve lawyers, your executive team, or other people — including their emails, phone numbers, or the preferred channels of contact. It is best to have this in your playbook, so you don't wake up on a Sunday with your company in the news, unaware because something was mishandled by a moderator who had no guidance.

Once again, this is not an endless or exhaustive list. You will need to add or modify as you see fit for your community, and commit to reviewing it at least yearly. You may also need to go to a very dark, pessimistic place for some of these situations. Many of the contents will be your "worst-case scenario," and you will want to involve the essential people in your company in building this.

I should add, the playbook can have positive elements too. How do you celebrate birthdays, weddings, births, graduations? Remember, the main goal of creating this document is to have consistent messaging, so there is no confusion, blatant favouritism, or bias. It also provides you with a great way to create memorable moments. Maybe, for example, the situational playbook states that, if you are made aware that it's someone's special birthday (e.g., they're turning 30,) a congratulatory e-card is sent out by the team.

How to Manage Moderators

Moderator management is a crucial part of any community manager's gig. So, besides working on the situational playbook and making sure they have the right resources, you may need to rely on experiences you've had managing others. Now, if you have never been a manager, that's not a problem. You will learn. Few people are born as a perfect human manager. However, let me share some things to consider when managing your moderation team, which I've learnt over time:

- Praise moderators for their work, but be very specific in the praise. Don't be afraid to share this particular praise with the moderation team.
- If a moderator makes a mistake (e.g., banning someone too quickly), deal with it privately. Clarify rules with the team without singling them out.
- When it makes sense, for a minor error, the community manager should take responsibility. This is to ensure the moderator doesn't lose credibility.
- It goes without saying, treat all the moderators the same (or as best as possible) to avoid the friction of one moderator bullying others.
- Have a process for moderators to voice concerns directly to you. Moderators should not be calling one another out or sharing their opinions on someone else's work publicly without first speaking with you and giving you the chance to address it.
- Make it clear that the community manager or forum administrator should be the one to regulate any issues or review any concerns about mistakes made. As noted above, this review and conversation should be private with that specific moderator, and there is no need to share that conversation with others when it's not relevant.
- To ensure continued learning, have regular meetings. Meetings should include any important encounters that can be learning opportunities, such as why a very active

community member was banned. You should share the rationale and steps that were taken by the moderator. This way, the team can see how things should be handled, and collectively, they can learn and build consistency from one another. It will also help you create the situational document we spoke of earlier.

As we wrap up this chapter on moderation, I want to state this again. You may make mistakes in your community moderator choices, or in managing moderators, but most times, it's fixable, and you learn a precious lesson. Every community manager has a story, so don't beat yourself up. Learn and move on.

As proof, let me tell you my own horrific moderator story from early in my career. I had a thriving community, but I noticed more troublesome content coming in while I slept. There was a very active and friendly member, who lived on the West Coast. I asked him if he'd mind keeping an eye on the community overnight. He was a night owl, and he could cover the community for me from 10:00 p.m. until 5:00 a.m. It was perfect.

And so, it was . . . for a couple of weeks. Then, one morning, I woke up, and all the content was gone. I was frantic. I emailed the moderator and asked what the hell happened. He told me, "I didn't want my username associated with any of the older posts I made, because I have a new job." I was flabbergasted. I told him I could easily have changed his username, which I did, and then I restored all the content from the hourly backups I kept. Nothing indicated to me this would happen. He was not very software savvy, but was an outstanding contributor. Because of this, I demoted his abilities, and thankfully he went back to being a great contributor the community needed. Eventually, I found someone who knew the software, had some better sense, and I gradually trusted them to take on a more significant role in moderating the community. It was a harsh, but valuable, lesson. Despite your best efforts, things will happen. It taught me to move slow, make sure the moderation team had good training, and to never assume...oh, and always have regular backups of community content.

Did this put me off having moderators? No. I learned valuable lessons, which I applied moving forward (many of which I have shared with you). Hopefully, some of the advice in this chapter helps you avoid a similar situation. However, please remember, you are human, and nobody is perfect in determining what another person will do. However, you can reduce the chances of issues if you have the right systems, training, and structure in place.

Chapter 20: Recognizing the Super Ones

I'll be honest with you. When I first started learning about super user programs years ago, I made the mistake of thinking most programs worked the same: You have a select group of people, who you identify as the most valuable people, and they get special access in your community. It turns out that it's not so cut and dried, and companies have many different ways of approaching super user programs.

Since I began with Vanilla in 2013, I have been exposed to super user programs with 5 to 45,000 members. I have seen programs managed by a sole community manager. I have seen programs handled by a vast customer experience team in conjunction with the community team. Also, in terms of rewards, I have seen all kinds of things. Some companies offer nothing more than member satisfaction of making better products. At the other extreme, I have seen super users added to a game in an animated form, or flown halfway around the world to the headquarters, given helicopter rides, and a luxurious dinner with the CEO at a five-star floating restaurant. There are lots of variety to programs, but no matter how they were constructed, most had the same core elements:

- Each program was hyper-tailored to their audience and reflected the company brand and culture.
- The company properly recognized contribution in some way, even if it was not always monetarily.
- It was clear how to get in, and even if you were not part of the prestigious program, there were

levels of appreciation for anyone striving to make it in.

- It was mutually beneficial to both parties. The super user gave time and effort. The company gave access, recognition, time, and value.

So, when should you launch yours? As with most things related to community, it depends. Each community is different, so I don't want to place a hard and fast rule in your mind. However, look at your goals and what you are trying to achieve with your community. I don't think it's wrong to plan to have one eventually, but I find it hard to build one until you have a better sense of what the actual community is like. In this way, you are dealing with a live community, rather than one on paper, and you have also a better handle on your needs.

Even with this uncertainty of when to start, it's undeniable that you should consider some sort of super user program at some point. I think this is why so many are eager to start right away. Here are just some examples of why a super user program can be so popular. They can:

- Tap into a potential living and breathing focus group (resulting in better products)
- Increase the ability to manage the community with fewer resources
- Help connect to your most passionate fans and recognize their loyalty in a way your competitors don't

However, with all the benefits, I would still caution, this is not something that always makes sense to have at the beginning. Remember SPAN framework? The "A" is for these programs — ambassador programs. Some people are very eager to start here first. I don't suggest you start your community with such a program unless you have already satisfied your community's original mission (i.e., the concept, and what you were trying to achieve for your business goals) — unless the goal is to create a space for super users from the start.

Regardless of when you begin, though, it's never too early to identify people who could be part of a program and recognize them with perks. This could be with a special badge and title in the community. Or you can step up the swag with handwritten thank you notes, chocolates or a t-shirt. However, don't stop there. The kind of programs we will be describing can be so much more. In the rest of this chapter, we will explore a more defined program that could eventually even run as its own separate community.

I want to also make very clear that this is different from an *influencer* program. Influencers have a following or may be mini-celebrities. However, super users usually have done the work and proven themselves as your loyal army. Do not confuse the two. If you have an influencer program, please tread carefully, by not lumping them together. In my view, your super users should always get a little more love. The super users are doing what they do for you, usually at expense of their time, and out of their own intrinsic motivation (i.e., they do it for *purpose* rather than the *purse* — a.k.a. money). Influencers usually do this as a career, a side hustle, or for extrinsic motivations.

If you think you're ready to build a super user program, let's go forward to see what it takes. However, before we begin, these are my assumptions:

- You have a community already built or some sort of platform for interacting with your community.
- You have some really active users, who you can talk with — and do so regularly — so you have a good sense of why they participate or spend time with your community.

If these are things you've yet to do, please go back to earlier parts of the book. We cover how to get here, including uncovering how to determine why members will put their best effort forward. Once we have these critical bits, only then can we build our super user program document. The following items should be included in your plan.

The Values and Goals of the Super User Program
Building something of significance is the primary goal, of course, but you should consider both the external and internal value of what you build. Why are you creating this program? You have to look at this value proposition from the company's and the member's perspective. Or in other words, why should your company invest, and why will members participate? You need buy-in for both of these cohorts. More than anything, I implore you to root your program in something straightforward for company success. For example, creating this program will save us from hiring focus groups and ensure we ship products with fewer errors, because our super users will be part of the QA (quality assurance) or beta process. They will, of course, be compensated and recognized for their help.

Also, the outward language to the membership should be more relevant to their interests: "Become a super user and be part of our cutting-edge future. We value your opinion and want your help testing the latest products before anyone else. Oh, and that's along with other snazzy perks like a t-shirt, exclusive discounts, and access to our team!" Wowza! Sign me up!

Roles and Expectations
What are the super users' roles, and what are the expectations? Consider this more as an internal document.

Will the super user have a role in influencing the roadmap? Does the role involve helping manage the community? Maybe the role is that they focus on the KB or write blog posts based on their experience. You want to be clear about the company's expectations of super users so you can communicate them properly in the public-facing recruitment document.

Identify Win-Win Rewards and Motivations

What are the benefits of participating? This is also usually tied to budget, in terms of what the company can commit to. This might also be impacted by the number of people in the program (fewer people should mean more), how important the program is to the company (I hope it is), and your community members' motivation.

In general, it is far more effective to lean into supporting those who do things for intrinsic motivations long term. Their main drive is their passion for the community or product. When people want to contribute innately, you have a potent force that you'll want to channel effectively. Generally, what they value is rewards that give them access/insight into the product/process and which have a direct impact on the direction of the company.

The other kind of motivation is extrinsic. This kind of motivation is doing something for external (monetary) rewards. You give them a task with a defined completion goal and a prize. Their primary motivator is the prize, and they are mercenaries. They may or may not have loyalty to your company, especially if these monetary rewards change or are lessened over time. Also, extrinsic motivation generally becomes less effective over a more extended period, even if the company has great rewards. People who don't feel personally invested in the community beyond rewards will eventually get bored and sometimes move on to the next company offering better "stuff."

Here is a way I like to think about these two motivations and the way rewards play their part. Those who are extrinsically motivated are offered a carrot to ensure they do something. Intrinsically motivated people get the carrot after they do something they were going to do anyway because they were self-motivated by their passion. Having a combination of both types of rewards and people in your program ensures a good balance.

Some ideas for reward inspiration for your program can include:

- Special community badges, ranks, or titles
- Access to unique content
- Access to special communication channels, like a private real-time chat
- Ability for people within your community to meet with the CEO or product teams
- Speaking opportunities for career development
- Discount or early access to products
- Unlocking of certain community platform features
- Company swag, like pens or hoodies
- All-out prizes like paid trips to company HQ

There are no hard and fast rules on rewards, and nothing is either right or wrong. However, don't feel you need to break the bank. People who want to be in your community should see the rewards as a surprise perk, not the reason to be there. Of course, no human is motivated purely by one motivation or the other, so a great program taps into both.

Community Curve

I wrote about the community curve earlier, and this is a great tool to visualize the "asks" you'll make of people to get a spot in your super user program. Is it a smooth curve, with a fair number of asks? Is the chasm too large? What should leaders be doing to make it into the program?

Selection Criteria

If you make your program public, you should detail the selection criteria for deciding who joins your MVP program — to some extent. They should not be added automatically. Every great program will have a pool of people who hit specific tangible goals, but who will be promoted to a *special* super user group because of something extra they've done. Just as when you select moderators, a super user should be someone you trust, because they will get access of some sort. You need someone mature, with a good temperament, and who uplifts your community.

Finally, along with selection criteria, consider what happens that would cause someone to fall out of the program. Most programs have a certain level of annual activity required, and some programs have an expiry date, with a set number of seats filled every year. The benefit of the expiry date or term limits is to ensure more people get the chance to be part of the program. You also encourage fresh ideas and excitement, and finally, you avoid people feeling entitled. I know of one super user program that has an expiry and a 1-year pause before a super user can apply again. This truly ensures they don't enable long-term memberships and also that they give everyone a chance.

This also doesn't mean you can't honour past super users either. You can consider a new grouping called Alumni Club, or some sort of distinguished grouping, that still recognizes their contributions and has some perks as well. The extra benefit of this alumni pool is that you are not alienating super users from coming back in the future, and they can reapply later. No matter what you decide, consider how you wish to construct things, so no one gets a free ride based on past performance.

Engage

Make sure your platform, or your system, has a way to identify potential candidates. Also, consider easy ways to encourage them. Maybe it's a helpful badge in the forum or a t-shirt you send along when they hit a milestone. I am aware of some communities that keep spreadsheets with this info to keep track – others use more sophisticated systems. They have a transparent point system — for example, looking at how many correct answers the applicant gave — and reviewing other aspects of their comments (including their temperament) before promoting them into the super users ranks.

Another possible way to handle things is a somewhat private super user group. When a potential super user is identified, you invite them to apply for the program. The application process is one way to ensure you get people likely to be more active in their participation, because it's something they seek rather than something awarded.

The group of applicants and people awaiting a spot can be in a special group, which can include the ability to be promoted should another super user need to step down or they become less active than required by your program guidelines. One community I am aware of has a super user group of five people, with 35 people on a list, waiting to take those slots. They rotate people out yearly, but after 12 months, people can resubmit to join. This makes sure no one becomes entitled, and it's fair to their most loyal fans.

Keeping it small also allows the company to afford exceptional perks.

I can't tell you how big or small your group should be. It's really up to you how you decide to handle it. Please just ensure that you have a defined system or process that is documented and clear to anyone working with you on moderating the community. They can assist in identifying those potential stars, especially if you have a larger community where it might not be as apparent.

Onboarding

Once someone is selected, it is crucial to create an onboarding process. This includes making it more special than just an email. Consider creating a welcome kit, which outlines expectations, maybe includes some swag, a handwritten letter from the CEO (or someone high up in the organization), and perhaps a video launch call or meetup. I cannot stress this enough, if you want your program to be unique, start with a wow moment. People notice these things, and if you are asking a lot from them, or it's hard to get into the program, you want to make sure they feel special right out of the box.

Also, if you're onboarding many new super users, consider assigning them a buddy who's already been a super user, who they can go to for any questions. That alumni group of past super users can be valuable to support those initiatives, so please consider it!

Create Special Spaces

Don't forget to create a unique space to connect with your super users. They need a place to share and get feedback from you, your team, and other program members. Consider regular video calls, access to a real-time chat system (like Slack), and other ways that give them direct and immediate access to communicate with one another and you.

Recognize Their Contribution Publicly

Besides giving them a special badge or honours in the online community, if it makes sense, consider spotlighting their contributions in newsletters, on the website, and other areas. It shows off your members' passion for your brand, and it's authentic. It's also an excellent way for them to feel their contributions have a real impact.

Create Opportunities for Leadership

Consider different opportunities you can give super user members for further leadership. For example, you can assign them particular tasks, like answering unanswered questions after 24–48 hours, leading the welcome of new users, starting discussions, or creating KB articles suggested by the community. Give them a bit of guidance, but let them run the program. In more mature programs, you may even consider paying for leadership course for them, that help them advance in their careers.

Keep Measuring and Giving Feedback

Ensure you have a mechanism to give regular and helpful constructive feedback — public praise and private criticism. Most people want to know how they are performing. Don't assume, because they don't ask, that they don't want to know.

With feedback also comes measurement. Have some way to measure how your super users are doing. Base these measurements on the most important goals of the program. You can also use this to help identify people who should join or may be at risk of rotating out.

If you have clear, measurable goals or objectives, people who lose their spot in a super user program should not be surprised. You will have communicated their performance.

You May Need Help

It depends on how ambitious you want your super user program to be, but the more complex and involved programs may require an additional head count. Many companies have a dedicated human resource just for their super user programs, separate from the community. For some companies, the community manager runs the super user program, and they deal only directly with the super users. Those super users, in turn, really run the community. Do what makes sense for you and your situation.

Lawyers

I cannot stress this enough — you *need* to involve a lawyer. Why? You have to ensure you construct the program in a way that follows the law and the jurisdictions you are in. super users are not employees, and you want to make sure you don't place your company in jeopardy. This doesn't even begin to cover potential bias/bribery prohibitions some employees/industries may have.

You will also want clear guidelines regarding content created for your community — along with ownership, copyright, and permission for your company to use it in other channels. So, yes, while going to a lawyer can slow things down or seem like a scary proposition, it is worth it to talk with legal counsel before an issue happens.

Almost every company I know has checked with their lawyers, and they still have programs — so it's certainly doable. You should account for the time required for a legal review in your launch plan, so it does not end up in delays or missing a deadline you may have shared publicly. You can choose to ignore this advice, and I know some do, but I would be remiss not to at least advise you to seek out some sort of legal check.

As you can see, there are lots of elements to a super user program. When done right, it adds so much to your community. However, I caution you to take your time to get the proper structure in place. It doesn't mean you aren't identifying potential members even before you launch. It just means you want your program to be meaningful and have something behind it. As the ol' saying goes: "You only get one chance at a first impression!" Now let's go out there and build something super!

Chapter 21: From the Bench to Starter

When I was a teenager in high school, I was on the badminton team. I was easily second string (maybe third, if I am honest). I sat on the bench. Our team made it to the provincial qualifiers. Even though I had not played any matches, I was always there, rooting for the team, and trying hard to get better during practice. On the day of the provincial qualifier, our star singles player got hurt, and I had to play for our team, or we would have had an automatic forfeit. I was petrified. I met my far superior opponent. He played at a badminton club in the city regularly. I was a kid who played in the backyard, and likely only made the team because I showed up and they needed to fill the slot.

I'd love to give you a heroic story about how I won, but the truth is, I lost very quickly. My team was very supportive and cheered me on, and in the end, even if I wasn't the star player, I, for once, really felt like part of the team. I scored a couple of points and did my best to be competitive. Even though I lost, it was a good experience. I got excellent pointers from the coach, and my game got better too. If nothing else, it was a good life lesson about being patient with yourself.

This is why I just embarrassed myself in my own book. I don't know what kind of situation you will find yourself in. Maybe you have to start from scratch or maybe you need to take over from someone else who was a star. We spent a good part of this book learning about how to start but what if but if you find yourself taking over as this type of accidental community manger? This scenario can be challenging even an expert, especially when we need to step into someone else's shoes. So, know this: if you find yourself taking on a new community role and you're brand new, give yourself a break. Don't try to be the old community manager. Have the patience to mould your raw talent for connecting people and building spaces into the community builder I know you can be. It's also tough to walk into someone's spot, but you have to do it your way and be open to learning how to be better.

Also, as much as I'd love to give you all the answers, it's not possible. The best thing I can do is provide you with advice on the three most common scenarios when taking over an existing community from another community manager.

You Inherit the Community and the Outgoing Community Manager Is Available to Help

This is usually the best scenario. If they have any sense of professionalism, most community managers care about their community, even if they're leaving the position. In this case, you will need to know who the key members in the community are, who can be trusted, what projects are in the works or were planned, and a general idea of the community and its tone. You will also hopefully get a copy of any playbook/situational playbooks and governance documents already created — so you don't have to start from scratch.

Depending on the circumstances of their departure and their own ability, they may not have created or left behind any helpful materials. It happens. However, if they did leave behind documents, or you have the opportunity to meet with them before they leave, I suggest you shadow them. Learn as much as you can, and hopefully, they will be willing/open to be called on after they leave. You may want to see if they can work as a contractor/coach as you get up to speed.

As much as you will shine in your own way, hopefully, they leave you with something to build on. If none of this applies, let's go ahead to the next scenario.

You Inherit the Community and the Community Manager Is Gone But Left Behind Notes

If you don't know the community manager, or they are gone when you take over, the hope is they left some sort of documentation. I would still try to reach out to them but proceed with caution if the termination of their employment was acrimonious. If you're not able to connect with them, take what they left and head into "listening mode" to see if the notes match up with your own impressions. I also encourage you to introduce yourself to the community, be as transparent as you can about the transition, and explain you'll now be on this journey together.

As a community member and builder, the biggest misstep you can make is when a long-time community leader disappears without some sort of acknowledgement, or if possible, an explanation. Your community should be about building relationships and transparency. Pretending your successor did not exist does not help set you on a good path.

If they were horrible, please refrain from bashing or bad-mouthing them. Just be clear it's a new chapter, and you're excited to be there. Be wary of any members "willing to help" with the transition. Indeed, some people are helpful, but some volunteers could have an agenda that may not reflect the needs or goals of the community. So, tread carefully (and I'll have more on that in a moment.) If you have no records or anything, go ahead to the next scenario.

You Inherit the Community and Have No Support

Sadly, if you landed here, this is not a surprise. You are likely the accidental community manager thrown into the firepit. I won't sugarcoat it — it's not easy. You'll need to canvas the company to find out if anyone knows *about* the community and be a detective to figure out who is who *in* the community. As in the prior scenario, proceed in a listen mode. If the community was on their own for a while, I might recommend delaying your announcement about taking over the community until you have a better sense of things. Once you do make your presence know, as I mentioned earlier, be wary of any offers from members offering to be moderators until you have your bearings.

I know this scenario is tough. Keep reading for advice on how to learn more about your inherited community.

The Total Shit Show

Now I want to add an extra element before we move forward. What happens if you inherit a community that — let's be honest, because it *can* happen — is a total shit show? Maybe it's a dead community, with no activity, or it's overgrown with spam and self-promotion due to neglect. What can you do?

Some people shut things down, and some people just delete and restart. Some people slog their way through and continue to build sandcastles by the ocean. So how can you, the community newbie, deal?

If you're part of the community space long enough, sadly, you'll see or participate in one or many of those outcomes. It can be hard and painful to see something loved turn into a festering pool of turds. Most times, when I have seen a community in shambles, it's directly correlated to organizational neglect. So now, if you find yourself in the role of community lead for a neglected community, you have some decisions to make.

Unless it's a completely toxic and unsalvageable place, I am not in favour of deleting and restarting without doing some work first. So, what's the plan? Here is how I would tackle the transition step-by-step. Modify as needed for whichever of the above inheritance scenarios you find yourself in:

Step 1: Research Phase

In all cases, before you announce your presence, spend some time inspecting the community, looking at the stats. What should you look at?

- What are the topics people are passionate about?
- What are the taboo/controversial topics (e.g., did your company do something that could inflame passions)?
- Who are the key/active members?
- Who are the troublemakers? (Has anyone been given warnings or been marked as a troll, but not banned?)
- How do members like to communicate (e.g., with GIFs or sarcasm) and are they helpful or supportive?
- Why do you think people are there?
- Who are some key internal staff or former community managers that can you interview to share their insights?
- Is the technology holding you back (can it control spam or do you lack moderation tools)?

Don't spend an endless amount of time on this. It should take about a week to get a sense of things.

Step 2: Announce You Are There

Once you have some information about the community, it's time to introduce yourself. Try to be as transparent as possible about the transition. Ask for time but keep a positive tone, letting members know that you are excited to be on the journey and learn together. Be authentic too. If that's not your style, adapt it to your own. The main thing is to make sure the community knows it's not been abandoned.

Again, you may be approached by members offering to help. I would politely thank them but not give them access to any moderation tools. However, feel free to use it as an opportunity to chat with them (in the next phase) and learn about the community.

Step 3: Information Gathering from "Members"

I have placed "members" in quotes, because some members may have left. You want to look at *all* the members — those who are active and those who *were* engaged and left the community. Now is the time to talk to members directly and understand their needs, wants, and motivations for using the community firsthand. This is also the time you can match up their answers with what the eager volunteers may have told you. The real goal is to get a firsthand sense of the community. Don't make any promises or plans. Be clear you are in learning mode.

If this is a B2B community, the main issue can be cliques or the shunning of "others," so be sure to include a variety of groups, nationalities, and backgrounds to speak to. Don't stay in your bubble, because it could just reconfirm company bias, especially if something is in dire need of fixing.

Step 4: Plan for Changes and Request Feedback

This is where you can take what you've learned and decide what you want to do. What changes in the guidelines need to be made? Who may need to be warned or banned? Do you need to restart the online community from scratch? Hopefully, during the interview process, you sussed out some trusted community members whose words match their public actions in the community – of being truly helpful stalwarts. I would ask them for feedback on your plan in confidence. If they are former members, I would ask if your planned changes would get them to recommit to becoming involved again.

Step 5: New Boss, New Rules

As you plan, I think it's a good idea to be transparent with the community — just as you were with the intro. Don't be shy to tell them that a new plan/community review is coming. The tone is not to come off as if you're a strict authoritarian, but let them know that someone new is now in charge. Also be clear regarding a date for such an announcement — this is especially important if you have to clean up the community of troublemakers/content, etc.

When that date comes, announce it again and point to the changes. Be open to constructive criticism, and give people a chance to speak their minds. However, also don't be shy about showing troublemakers the door. It's your job to manage the community.

Step 6: Status Check

Give yourself, at most, a quarter to review where you were and where you are now. Did things improve? Check back with your earlier interviewees. Do community calls. Make modifications as needed, and continue these check-ins at least yearly, or as frequently as you feel it makes sense.

I hope the above list helps you transition from one community leader to the next. I know every situation is different, but all you can do is try to do your best.

For those facing a total community mess, you may have no choice but to shut it down. However, I can say, in all my years working with B2B communities, most communities are not total shit shows, but suffering from one of the following factors (if not all):

- A horrible concept (e.g., too product-focused and not member-needs-focused).
- A lack of organizational focus or planning (the community is an afterthought or reactive in the planning).
- No dedicated human resources (without supervision, trolls run rampant because guidelines are not enforced).
- No consideration of the needs of community members, focusing instead on KPIs (in other words, members don't know why they should participate, because the value was never communicated or obvious).

In my mind, these are all fixable, and I think this book has many solutions for you. Only you and your team can decide the community's fate, and I certainly can't make you make the effort or spend the resources to save it. I can, however, provide advice and my experience to help. In the next chapter, let's learn some ways to turn around a quiet or dead community.

Chapter 22: What if My Community is Dead?

A community almost never dies. I purposely used the word "community" and not "forum" or "online community" in the title of this chapter. Why? Communities rarely die — but forums can. People will almost always seek bonds with others or cluster around ideas, causes, and passions that matter to them. They may just no longer use the space you've created. It happens. Usually, this occurs when there is a vast chasm between what your company cares about and what the members care about. If your community forums don't cater to "what's in it for them," your members will simply cease caring about your space and find one that does.

This is not the only reason forums can die. It might be a lack of focus or attention paid. Sometimes, the community gets abandoned, and the company just ignores it. However, if you're reading this book, I assume this is something you are actively trying to fix. This chapter is for you.

First, I'd like to review some signs that indicate your forum is dead or dying. What are the things you can look at? What are the things to guard against? Is all Adrian going to do is ask me questions? No, I promise. I will also give you some ideas on how to turn it around. Sound fair? Let's go!

Note that the following signs can be a cause for concern, but the more you see, the more concerned you should be. Some are warning signs of bad things to come, and some might be things you observe from a former community manager, if your role is now to come in as a saviour.

More Discussions Than Comments

If you see more discussions than comments, I worry that the sense of community (i.e., caring for others) is relatively low. It's essentially people yelling and no one responding. I always like to see 2X comments-to-discussions. It's normal when first launching a community, that there will be some discussions without comment, but the expectation is that this will turn around over time, with hard work, a plan, and the right environment. At the very least, every discussion should get one comment — even if it's just from you in the early stages.

Lots of Questions and No Answers

Similar to the above — but almost more painful — is a forum where people ask for help, and no one answers them. Sure, people might not comment on a discussion because they have nothing to add. Or maybe the questions are too hard for them to respond to. However, if people in the community are outright not answering, or even reacting, it's a potential warning that your community lacks a sense of belonging or empathy.

No Reaction and Content Consumption Down

On some online community platforms, people can react to content with a like or a thank you button. Those were added to reduce the clutter of threads of people writing one-word "thank you" posts. If people in your community are not taking the time to do even that, things are not looking good. In your analytics, you can also see these metrics: pages per visit, page views, overall sessions, and time on site. If all these are down, you are heading to a funeral, if not dead already.

New Users Aren't Signing Up

A community needs new blood. However, measuring how many people join is a vanity statistic. For example, why celebrate if 100 new people join your community, but they do nothing? Are your company goals being improved positively by this growth? If nothing else changes, does it matter?

Or even worse, what if these people are signing up and they never return? Is your promise of what's inside not being adequately fulfilled? Immediate abandonment after sign-up is a quick tell. This is why I regularly test the sign-up as a new user. I come to the community as a guest and go through the whole process to ensure there are no blockers. I also want to ensure that what we show, or promise, before sign-up aligns with what's inside (i.e., that we deliver). If people are signing up, they are showing interest in your offer, so find out where the leak is happening. If you really get stuck on why people are disappearing, try adding an on-exit survey, or mouse recording analytics for additional datapoints.

Now, what if people are just not signing up at all? For example, you had a bunch every day, and now it's one member per month. I won't lie, this is the kind of change that is concerning. Maybe you need to look at your analytics and see the historical sources of signups. Was it the blog or an email promotion? Perhaps it's a link that disappeared from your home page? However, we should note more mature communities have a slower rate of new members. For this reason, the rate of new users is not a helpful metric. However, drastic changes in trends are a concern.

What are other ways you can be looking at this? Consider the ratio of new users who join, actively participate, and engage the community. This can either be by creating, reacting, or consuming content. If you have a ton of new users and the activity is close to zero, this is a problem. Watching this trend is one of the health metrics I monitor to see how things are going. Poor consumption and engagement from new users will have a significant long-term impact on the KPIs that matter to the business.

Top Members Are Gone/Less Active

Every community will have some very active members. Hopefully, you know them well. If you inherited your community, you should look up who these people are. If these people have stopped participating — or you see them being less active — this could be something to check on. One active member gone is not a cause for alarm, especially in the B2B space. Things happen, people change jobs, or priorities change. In this case, I'm referring to a wholesale disappearance or reduced activity by a large part of this cohort. It's a signal they lost reasons to care.

Active Users and Activity are Down and Constant

A forum heading to a death spiral will see active users participating less and general forum activity grinding to a halt. Some communities have spikes when they have releases or events, but if those historical spikes stop (or are not as significant), this is also a sign that something is happening you'll want to investigate.

The Moderation Team is Not Present or as Active as They Were

I'm not talking about you; you're here. I'm referring to your moderators. Look at the moderator or community accounts and see when they last logged in. Do the timelines make sense with the decline? For example, it might show neglect if the community manager left in June but last logged in

March. The same with the moderation team. One moderator not being active is not a trend, but most of them not caring is a concern. This could mean a lack of leadership before you arrived, or the wrong moderators were there to start with.

Senior Management Not Aware

This one is more for you community managers joining a company or taking on forums, who learn that senior management was unaware there *was* a forum. In the end, this is a channel for customers, and if it's being neglected at the highest levels, it's likely not a good sign. Well, the good sign is that you're there now. Nonetheless, it also probably means this space has been neglected, and it's likely the customers know that too.

General Neglect

Once again, I am looking at the newbie taking over. If you see banners on the site announcing an event from last year or pinned topics about spring in the dead of winter, this is neglect.

Another sign of neglect would be generic cut-and-pasted comments to almost all discussions. If you see that, it's clear the former community team didn't even care to take the time to personalize responses, or in other words, they saw community interaction as a "chore." It's a warning sign of bad things to come and something to guard against. We never want to get so complacent that we copy and paste similar responses to every post. People notice.

Other signs of general neglect: trolls are running rampant, spam posts, tons of links to other sites being promoted, and the moderation queues are full of things to review.

The Company is Embarrassed

This is where the company is aware of the community, but rather than fixing things, they remove links to it. It can only be found by those with bookmarks or by searching Google. In other words, there is no direct door from the company website to the forums. Be aware that I am not talking about the situation where a company neglects to add your community link to their menu options. I am talking about actively removing it to hide it. Their goal is to choke the oxygen to the community.

Wow, what a list! Don't worry, though, Our goal now is to help you revive things! So how to turn it around? This is the time I have noticed some companies think platform change is needed. Sometimes it is, but most times, the cause is not the platform. It's the strategy tactics, the messaging, the concept, or the approach. Sometimes people link a new platform as the impetus for change, but really, that's not what is needed (in most cases). Let's now talk about turning things around.

Getting back on track is never easy, and I want to be honest that sometimes it's not always possible. However, the following are the steps I would take to approach things (and much of it is similar to the chapter "From Bench to Starter" – the main difference is your starting point).

Step 1: The Audit

This is the hardest part — getting the courage to look at things honestly and make a change. Try not to start with assumptions, but look at this as a fact-finding mission. You may learn something you were not expecting by leading with curiosity.

To start, here are the avenues I like to explore. Remember, this is just fact-gathering at this point:

Workflow

- Are we making it easy to sign up?
- What is the onboarding messaging workflow? Does the onboarding invite them with action-oriented tasks (e.g., requesting they share a tip or advice, asking what they are most excited to learn, or what people they want to connect with)?
- How easy is it to start a discussion or comment?
- Have we clarified how to use the platform (e.g., explained the features)?

Audience

- Are we clearly advertising the online community to our audience?
- What other touchpoints do we have to remind our audience or gain new community members (e.g., newsletters)?
- Have we spoken to our community audience about their experiences, needs, and interests? Don't ask them what the community can do for them, but rather what problems they need help solving or what resources would help them succeed in their goals.
- Have we reached out to those who left to find out why?

Community Data

- Is there a mismatch to the content? Are people searching for content our community does not have?
- Are people interacting with our content? If so, which content?
- Have we applied segment, data-based, on-job function, or experience to see a trend?
- Do we survey them when they close their session to see if they achieved their goal or how we can improve?

Step 2: The Theory

Once you have done the audit, now is the time to build your theories to test them. Maybe you realize the sign-up process is too complicated. Maybe you figure out that the content is a mismatch to the searches. Perhaps you have no data. Write down all your theories — we will soon confirm them.

Step 3: The Interviews

This is where you take your theories and approach your potential audience and community. The audience is the people who *could* join your community. Now is also time to confirm your hypothesis. Maybe you think the concept is poor. It could be too broad (i.e., not focused enough), or it could be so niche that nothing is compelling or intriguing about it to your more extensive audience. You will only know that once you talk to people. Remember, don't impose your vision of the community. You want to be building it *with* them. Listen and ask. Focus on their needs. Not the community platform or technology. This can be changed. You need to know what they care about.

This is not to say that you need to ignore technology. If you are stuck long term with a software you don't like, or if you learn the platform is a big issue, you can do user testing. This can be done by either having people come in or by using a tool to watch how people interact with your community. Set up the tasks you want and have them talk aloud. Ask customers, or potential customers, unfamiliar with your online community to complete specific tasks. See what happens and note their frustrations. Having this first-hand evidence can also help you make the case for a software change.

I should note to not only take customer community feedback at face value. It's undoubtedly important to know how they feel, of course, but don't feel restricted by it. Your plans may go beyond their asks or be better long term. Sometimes you may have to read between the lines. Once again, a good way to stay focused is to home in on the problems they are trying to solve and what they need to be successful. Don't get hung up on platform. Understand first, then solve.

Step 4: The Plan

Once you have the data, start to build a plan. Some questions to ask:

- Do we need to change the concept?
- Does the community platform need a new theme?
- Does it have the features we need?
- Can we add guides, new workflows, or simpler sign-up forms to get people in?
- Do we need to invest in people to help?
- Do we need Dev or IT help to implement changes?
- Can we get the budget for these changes?
- Does our organization have the will to change?

With hope, your organization has the willingness to change. This can be one of the hardest things to overcome, but aim to show the value and impact by choosing KPIs and goals which matter to stakeholders. Generally, if you have solid objectives that impact the bottom line, especially in terms of dollar impact, you can get the support you need.

Before you present that plan to management, figure out the must-have vs. nice-to-have items to get back on track. Get estimates on the timeline to fix or implement those changes, along with any budget. Presenting a clear and thoughtful plan to your management team is a crucial step for buy-in.

Once you have their commitment, and only then, you'll want to communicate with those you spoke with and your community that change is coming. Be as transparent and authentic as you can. Ensure they know the specific date and ask them to "save the date." I've even seen companies mail out paper invites with stickers and swag. This is your big relaunch party, and it's a *huge* event — so build that excitement!

Step 5: The Feedback

Before you do your major relaunch, consider bringing in those you interviewed to get their feedback. You'll want these allies with you on the relaunch. Hopefully, if they care enough to share with you — and in a meaningful way — they care enough to see you succeed. A reward in the platform, such as a badge or special access to content, can be an excellent way to recognize them or thank them for their help.

Step 6: Relaunch

This is it, the relaunch day. Accept that, even with the best intentions and plans, things go wrong. Nonetheless, if you've listened, tested, and iterated, you will see the success you seek. Make sure now not to take your eyes off the community. Continually ask for feedback, hold calls with your community's best users, and keep staying engaged and looking at the data. I know you can do it!

As I mentioned earlier, sometimes you just fail. Communities rarely die, but sometimes the spaces for the community don't work. All you can do is listen and create the best space for them. Sometimes it's also just a matter of timing — for example, the space was built too soon, or you missed your opportunity. It happens. If anything, my most significant failures led to my best community-building lessons. It's okay to make mistakes, but try your best to learn from them. I believe you've got this! Do you know why? Because you care enough to read this book, so go out there and wow us!

Chapter 23: DEIB — A Conversation to Have

No book about community would be complete without a conversation about diversity, equity, inclusion, and belonging (DEIB). Now I know, before we even start, some may ask: "How can a white cis male write about (DEIB)?" A couple of thoughts on this. DEIB allyship is important. If you are part of a dominant group, it's important to use this position to champion DEIB initiatives.

The other thought I had, especially if you're learning about community for first time, I wanted to provide insight on the topic especially how it applies as you build your community. We all have biases — and the more privileged you are, the harder you need to work at guarding against them. Those who have had terrible experiences because of their race, age, ethnicity, sexual orientation, may also bring biases with them. It's a hard balance to get right. If you have too much hyper-awareness you could overcorrect if not careful.

So, what can you do? My experience has taught me that you should start by leaving your ego behind and be open to learn, lead with empathy, and seek input from others. It means co-creating and consulting with others in groups in your community before you make important community choices. It also means to listen hard when people raise concerns to you. This is the challenge I give to you: Seek out the opinions and the feedback of as many groups as you can on decisions that impact the community. Have those difficult conversations; your community will be better for it.

Please also tread with caution as you seek insight. For example, please don't accost your one colleague or community member of colour with all the requests for the "Black opinion." Don't ask the one person with a visible disability in your company to represent all people with a disability. This is not the way. It can create a perception of tokenism - making it seem like the only reason you want their opinion is because they are hearing impaired, gay, or a BIPOC (Black, Indigenous, and people of color). I recommend, rather, that you bring in a diverse group of people from your community, so the pressure is not on one person — or better yet hire a DEIB consultant or seek those out doing great work like Shana Sumers, Ashleigh A. Brookshaw, Victoria Cumberbatch or Marjorie Anderson. If you want to create great community experiences, it's imperative you ask or seek help. Making assumptions is where you get into trouble, even if you've had experiences which can inform you. Furthermore, getting other perspectives can only help to remove your own bias even if your own experience keeps DEIB top of mind. I applied this advice even for this chapter. I got the most input from my network to ensure I avoided any blind spots. Thanks to Carrie, Nichole, Marjorie, Ashleigh, Joanna and others for your important feedback that made this chapter so much better than the original.

There is another reason DEIB should matter to you and your company: When you don't account for DEIB, you exclude, even if not on purpose. It doesn't matter what your intentions are. There are things you could be doing which is sending a message to some of your community that they are not welcome. Don't you want your community to help as many people as possible? Of course, you do! So, let's do the work!

The following is a non-exhaustive list to get you started on the things to consider and review as you build your community:

- Be intentional in recruiting and actively nurturing a space where all identities are celebrated.
- Consider how your community showcases diversity. Make sure it's not a token diversity, highlighting your one member of colour. Make sure the photos used in your community marketing materials have a diverse set of people.
- If your audience is international, reconsider the acronyms, slang, jargon, or examples used.
- Be mindful to use gender-neutral language — drop the "Hey, guys" for "Hello, all" or "Hello, y'all." Use something that aligns with the tone of voice for your community.
- Ask all members for preferred pronouns when they sign up. We want to normalize the pronouns for a more equitable experience for non-binary folks or folks who chose to present differently.
- Make sure you have content written by people of different points of view.
- Review Web Content Accessibility Guidelines (WCAG) and ensure your platform, and your spaces, are accessible for people with all kinds of abilities.
- Consider how various abilities will consume your email, video, and audio content — can you get live transcription services, people to sign, are you adding descriptions to images?
- Consider that not everyone has the same access to technology or high-speed internet. For example, consider creating a light version of your community experience which is easier to

load or a way people can participate via email to be part of the conversation.

- Don't ignore larger issues — in the news, for example — that could affect members. Offer them the space to speak — or not. Make them feel protected and supported, even if it's their choice to remain silent.
- Collect feedback or do interviews on a regular basis on how you can do better.
- Ensure you have clear community guidelines on expected behaviour and act swiftly when someone breaks the rules.
- Remember that good intentions aren't an excuse for harmful actions. If someone does something that harms another member on purpose, or by accident, the end result is the same, no matter the intent? Don't let "intent" be an excuse for bad behaviour. Actions should have consequences.

I know the above is not an endless list; it never was going to be. However, I hope as you read through, it helps you develop a proper mindset for the work to be done. Being open and acting on DEIB will help create a better space for your members and, in turn, even better communities. If you want to delve deeper on the subject, you should check out the writings of Robin D'Angelo, Ruchika Tulshyan, Desiree Adaway and Ijeoma Oluo – hat tip to Carrie Melissa Jones for these suggestions. I hope you continue your learning journey on this topic beyond this book. It's something we can all benefit from doing no matter our community building experience.

Chapter 24: Continued Success — What Does It Take?

Friends, you made it. Your community is going along, the community numbers look great, but now we must consider the following: What does it take to keep going? We know the community project is never finished, and yet I have seen so many people fall prey to "unforced errors" — simple avoidable mistakes that can lead to losing fantastic progress made.

For the uninitiated, or those confused, an unforced error is when you make a preventable mistake — by your own actions. Usually, it happens in sports, like when someone mistakenly scores on their own net or runs the wrong way in a football game.

As we come closer to the end of this book, I know I won't be able to alert you as you go off-course. So, to help, and maybe as a checklist for you on your journey, I'd like to review some things that can happen, which, if not corrected, can lead to more significant challenges in the future.

If there is one chapter I would recommend you revisit once you complete this book, this is it. It's my list of things to ensure your continued success.

Avoid unforced errors by:

- Staying engaged in the community and communicating
- Revisiting your strategy and goals quarterly
- Checking the new user path and onboarding quarterly
- Ensuring community visibility continues on digital platforms and within the organization

- Talking, listening, and soliciting feedback regularly from the community
- Looking at the data, taking action, and testing new things

Below are some longer thoughts on the list above.

Connections and Sharing

It's so crucial for you to keep yourself and your community visible. For some, being a wallflower is a natural position. Your community needs you to be its PR team within the company. I know it's hard to brag, but your community needs you to tell everyone, as much as you can, about what the community is doing to impact the business in a good way.

Furthermore, you need to maintain those connections with your business allies, especially if you want, or need, their help creating community content. There are other benefits, though. Not only will you continue to get valuable intel, but you'll ensure you are in the know, so your community continues to be aligned with the company's goals. Allies can also enhance and help you with your community goals — if it benefits them toward company objectives.

Strategy and Goals

You did the work on strategy and goals. It does not end when you place pen to paper. You need to constantly review, tweak, and iterate. It's also not enough to agree this makes sense, but plan for the times you will actually do the work. To me, the minimum is once a quarter. Take a breath and review where you are and assess. You cannot keep running without taking a look at what you've done and where you are. Maybe there are opportunities you are missing. Perhaps you are doing things that are simply time-wasting or not working. Protect yourself by taking the time to review and look at things.

Onboarding Paths

I can't tell you how many community projects I have worked on that forget this simple step. Early on, when they launch, they spend a significant amount of time with the onboarding process and then they never revisit. As sure as the sun rises, things change. You will have new content, extra resources, or you'll learn how to do things better, that you will want to incorporate into your onboarding. Set a date at least once a quarter to experience your onboarding as a new community member and see what happens. What are the stumbling blocks? Are all the things triggering? Is it compelling? What are you missing?

There is another reason to do this audit and checkup. Sometimes things break, and no one reports it. Sometimes things break, and only you may notice. Sometimes your IT or marketing team moves a link and doesn't tell you. Sometimes a resource has outdated information. Sometimes you totally forget — what made sense once doesn't make sense six months later.

Don't be shy to get feedback from new members. Your original members may have had a clearer understanding than those discovering your community for the first time. Maybe they have suggestions to make things better?

I have seen broken onboarding totally derail a great community. Don't forget to make sure your first impressions are always the best impressions!

Visibility

We talked about having visibility of your community within the organization, sharing wins, and letting people know how your community is doing. I believe no one will tell your story if you don't share it. However, there is another aspect to community visibility you need to ensure, and this is more tangible.

You want to make sure the link to your community is just as prominent, if not *more* so, than links to social media or other channels. You want to make sure your community is part of any newsletter when it can be or included (if it's a support space) on any recording customers hear when they call or get an autoresponder from a ticket.

Continued Presence

Sometimes we get complacent. The community is running along, so we feel we can slip into working primarily on the behind-the-scenes stuff. However, I am a big proponent of staying present. Sure, you may have great volunteers, moderators, or staff, but you need to stay engaged. You should also be visible enough that these teams can come to you if there are problems, and you have a general sense of the culture. I've always been mindful to check in with comments or discussions at least monthly, even in the communities where my daily attention was not needed. I like to keep up with the pulse of the community. Firsthand knowledge is an excellent addition to any reporting your staff may give.

Don't Stop Gathering Feedback

Over time it can feel like things are fine. No one is complaining. This may be true, but I've found, the longer you manage the community, the bigger your blind spot can become. You can also easily fall into "this is what we've always done." Challenge yourself to keep soliciting feedback from your members. Have monthly feedback calls or surveys (with a contact option). Make sure there is a clear way you can talk to members about the feedback and get clarity. Don't assume everything is perfect if you never hear anything bad. Sometimes you need to ask to learn — the grain in the shoe is not uncomfortable until you walk a couple of miles. Make sure you get to those minor annoyances before they get bigger.

Do More Than Look at Data

It can be easy to get complacent month to month with reports. Make sure you do more than *look* at data . . . take action. Is there content that we could be creating from searches? Is a popular category now slowing? Is there a potential for a new category around a hot topic? It also does not need to be based on content metrics. It's nice to look at data around the design and spruce things up. Add a splash of colour, new offers in the sidebar. Your community is a living space. Use the data to enhance the experience. Test new ideas and show you still care!

      That's all . . . well, kind of. I could keep going, but I guess my main piece of advice for the future is the following: community-building is not "set and forget." Creating and maintaining an amazing community is not something with an end date, but it's a hell of a fulfilling and fun proposition. Hopefully, I've given you some ideas to be successful going forward today, tomorrow, and into the future!

Chapter 25: Listen to Your Health

This last chapter may be the most important one I will ever write, especially for those doing community-building work. If you enter into this career path, as rewarding as it may be, it can also be the most emotionally draining career. As someone who is always "on" for the community, it can be hard when you come down. It's normal in those quiet moments to get sad or feel exhausted. I just want you to know you aren't alone. It happens. Finally, as a quick disclaimer, I'm not a medical professional, and this is not to give you medical advice either. These are just my thoughts on the subject. If you need help, please reach out to a professional. Asking for help is not a weakness. It shows self-awareness of your limits.

The hardest and most important thing I had to learn as a community builder was to learn how to respect my personal downtime and plan for it. You need time to disconnect. Lock away those digital devices and reconnect to the physical world. You need to discipline yourself to listen to your mind, body, and soul to take the breaks you need. I'm also speaking as someone who learned these lessons the hard way.

In my mid-twenties, I was working in a very high-stress environment. Although, if you asked me at the time, I would have lied and said I had everything under control. However, one day, I had trouble breathing, and then I broke out into a rash. Sometimes I would get unexplained painful headaches, when I had never had headaches like that before. There were moments I thought I was going to die. I was sent to a disease specialist by my company. They, too, were really concerned about my health. My father came with me, as I was subjected to numerous tests at the hospital. Was it a tumour? Was it an unknown disease I had gotten while travelling for the company? Was it something I might die from? Did I catch it soon enough? It was one of the scariest times of my life.

After a month, all the tests were finally done. I was called in to have a follow-up appointment at the doctor's office to get the results. My father came with me again. I knew if it was something terminal, I would not be able to drive home. I was getting ready to battle for my life. The doctor came into the room. I took a deep breath.

"Mr. Speyer, is your work stressful?" the doctor asked, looking over his glasses.

"It can be challenging, but I wouldn't call it stressful."

He stared at me as if I had just lied. I had.

"Sure, I know what you do, and where you work. I know you have lots of stress," he began, as he closed the folder with the stacks of paper. "As you know, you've had all these tests, and I can say with 100 percent certainty that you have nothing wrong. All the tests came back as normal. The only thing you have is a body reacting to stress."

I sat stunned, even as he continued to talk. I'm not sure what else he said. I looked at him and repeated. "You are essentially saying that all of this is in my head," I stammered, and then somehow added, "Are you saying that stress is causing these physical reactions?"

"Yes. It's 100 percent all from your inside," the doctor said firmly.

"Well, that has to change, and it will," I said with confidence.

I thanked the doctor, with my head spinning, and headed home. I can't tell you what happened, but something changed in my mind. I was relieved to know it was within my brain to control. I made changes to my life to protect myself and my health. I stopped working on weekends, and I made clear work/life separation. I learned to take joy in life in simple things, such as eating lunch or going for a walk.

And thus, within a month, "mysteriously," the breathing problems, aches, and rashes disappeared, just as the doctor predicted. I am also thankful to report they have never returned. It left me, thankfully, with a lesson on the importance of protecting myself and my soul, and it's something I hope to pass on to you. Your community is important, but if you don't take care of yourself, you can't take good care of them. Always take care of yourself first, listen to your soul, and watch for the warning signs to protect yourself.

Over the years, I have used some different strategies, and I wish to share them with you below. Use the ones that work best for you, or anything else not listed, as long as you put yourself first. So, without further ado, here is my non-exhaustive list of suggestions for self-care.

Mindfulness

This is something relatively new for me, calming myself via mediation, and centring myself to clear my mind. There are tons of books and strategies out there. I've also adapted it to be mindful of my feelings and experiences. To take the appropriate time to be actively aware with family and friends, and to be present and enjoy their company. In other words, when I am with my loved ones, I centre on them, and I push out thinking about work or problems. I give them 100 percent of my energy.

Digital Cleanse

If you follow me on social, you will see that I actively unplug from social media on weekends. I very rarely go online or on devices. I don't want to read emails or be interrupted digitally by anything. I think it's great to disconnect and read a book, work in the garden, and do tactile things.

Special Treats

In this case, I am not talking about cookies or candies (though I love them). I mean creating something to look forward to in your day — something not work-related. For me, it's baseball. When my favourite teams play (I have a couple), I know work stuff ends, and my focus goes to that. It could be Friday movie night, or board game Tuesday. Maybe it's family time, doing puzzles. Have something regular you can look forward to.

Quiet Time

When work is done, before I engage with my family, I shut down the computer. I give myself time to take deep breaths and exhale the day. Play some music. I take alone time to just reconnect and ground myself. As much as you want to give to your community, giving to your family is more important. Make sure to recentre yourself for them.

The No Judgement Zone

Find other community builders and have a regular chat without judgement. I am lucky to have many friends in the community-building space, and we all know the toll it takes. Sometimes just talking out your frustrations with these friends can be so energizing. You are not alone. Imposter syndrome is real. So is feeling like a massive failure or fraud — trust me, even the biggest names in the space feel like that. I created a biweekly call for Vanilla customers who are community-building, just so they have this kind of space too. I am lucky to be able to facilitate this. We all need somewhere to talk and just vent. Don't have a network yet? There are a couple of communities for community managers, or you can find others on LinkedIn. Seek those out — it's essential!

Journaling

If you are shy, this is something that can work. Every day, write about your day, what is upsetting you, and I also like to add what I am thankful for. It's so easy to fall into pessimism, and I found that pushing through the positive has helped my spirit so much. Look for the good things of the day, the things you learned, the goals you aspire to. It's a great thing to have a book of the amazing things in your life to look at when you're down, as a reminder.

Hobbies

This is a big one for me. I have lots of hobbies. Find something you are passionate about, direct your energy, and take your brain away. I love to collect stamps and read comic books. I play Magic: The Gathering. I enjoy a good game of Fortnite. I've already told you about my joy of baseball. I have friends obsessed with Lego, puzzles, gardening, chicken raising, curling, golf, and baking cakes. Whatever it is, make it something where you can get away from your work. You'd be amazed at what happens when you truly engross yourself in something other than your work. It will also make you a better community person to understand being passionate about something.

Taking Time Off

Some will tell you a community manager can't take time off. Indeed, some even like to joke that it's a myth. However, if you genuinely can't take time off, I suggest you are doing it wrong. You should be able to step away from your community for a week without issue. It's about following the advice of creating governance, playbooks, and situational guidelines. There is always someone at your company who can help monitor your community — seek and ask. And hopefully, you also have moderators who can keep an eye on things for you. I recall once, I was about to go on a cruise with my wife, and I was nervous about leaving the community. She's a nurse and can be very direct.

"Is there anything life or death in your community? If you don't take care of yourself, and you die, that's really the bigger problem." She was right. As someone who has seen her patients die, in some cases, in her arms, her perspective was necessary. I also had a good group of people watching things. Don't lose sight of the fact that, while your work is important, you need to take care of yourself. And while your community is important, you are *more* important. No one (with hope) will die because you take time off to care for yourself.

I guess some of you may need to hear it plainly from me: "You have my permission to take time off." Why? Because if you read this book, you've built systems to make it possible. And if you haven't yet, you know that you can and should. I can't undersell how important it is for you, your loved ones, and the larger community to ensure you are your best self. Please take the time to care for yourself. Listen to your body and soul, and ensure you use your time off. Everyone who matters at your organization should understand this — and if they don't, it's not the place for you.

That's all, folks! You're now ready for your community-building journey. I know you'll make me proud. Go out there and change the world! \o/

Epilogue

I had to just say a small final goodbye. I know this can seem so overwhelming. No one is expecting you to be an expert overnight. I can't tell you all the mistakes I've made in my life, career, and in community-building to get here. Things will never be perfect but accepting this is an excellent first step. How can you cope with that? Focus on the good in people, life events, situations, and output positive warmth and energy to others. All the great things in my life came when I realized that people would rather be around those with positivity. Be a positive spirit in your community. Be the connector. Be authentic. Be yourself. This doesn't even need to be a big change to who you are. The simplest change is to learn that you can control your reactions.

The best example of this is the following: A glass of milk is spilt by accident by someone at a table you are having dinner with, and it spills onto your pants.

You can choose to:

A. Be angry or upset. Yell at them for ruining your favourite pants and for their clumsiness.
B. Be sad for them and make them feel even more uncomfortable.
C. Laugh and tell them about the time you spilt wine on the CEO of your company. It's no big deal; you hated these pants anyway.

What person do you want to be? I want to be C whenever I can. I *choose* to be that person. Be that person too. We need more people like this in our world.

And so, with that, I need to, once again, thank you for making it this far. I'm genuinely humbled you've made it to these final words. I never thought they would be written, and I would get a chance to get them all out in such a book.

I hope my words have helped you on your journey, and I hope you share them with others. The best thanks I can receive is to have you tell others to get this book. Leave a review on Amazon, Goodreads, or any fine bookstore website. Tweet me your favourite passages or share them with me on LinkedIn. Finally, you can also find me at my website https://adrianspeyer.com — I'd love to hear about your community journey.

Thanks again to everyone who made it this far; you've made my dreams come true by reading this. May *your* dreams come true in such a spectacular fashion too. Onward to your success!

Acknowledgements

I was full of trepidation when I started writing this book in 2018. I was a frustrated author inside who had, over the years, attempted to write non-fiction and consistently failed to finish. However, something told me it would be different this time. I knew I needed to write all my experiences down because I had something to say. Also, I hadn't read the book I wished existed — a book from the point of view of the accidental community manager — so I wrote it myself.

Writing the book was an arduous task. It started with me writing every Friday morning before work. While I was making progress, it was moving slowly and becoming a bit of a joke with my friends. I was struggling to balance time to write with a monster, three-hour commute each day. Then Covid happened, and so did working from home. Out of this horrible plague came the hours I got back, the hours I needed to finish this book. My vacations became marathon writing sessions as I neared the end of the book. Along the way, I was encouraged by family, friends, and colleagues. They held me accountable and constantly asked, "how's the book coming along"?

So, I'd like to take a moment to thank the following people for their support. First, I want to start with Melanie Attia, who encouraged me to keep at it in the early days and Derrick Eason, who gave me initial feedback on the first outline.

As I wrote this book, I had countless interactions that impacted me and this manuscript in incalculable ways. I would be remiss not to give a hat tip to the following people for their time, their inspiration, and their friendship:

Amanda Petersen, Angie Coleman, Ashleigh A Brookshaw, Beth Arritt, Bill Johnston, Brian Oblinger, Christina

Brashear, Dani Weinstein, David Spinks, Diana Morgan, Emily Gothschlack, Erica Kuhl, Esther Heide, Erika Brookes, Evan Hamilton, Haya El Masri, Holly Firestone, Ike Nwabah, Jay Nathan, Jean Olivier, Jeremy Meiss, Jessica West, Joanna Luth, Jodie Meier, John Ragsdale, Jono Bacon, Kara Adams, Kevin Boyce, Lincoln Russell, Luc Vezina, Marjorie Anderson, Matthew Revell, Matthieu Aubry, Mike Ellis, Nuala Cronin, Patrick Groome, Rachel Happe, Richard Millington, Sarah Judd Welch, Sarah Robinson-Yu, Scott Genzer, Shana Sumers, Shauna McClemens, Tanja Laub, Tessa Kriesel, Todd Burry, Todd Nilson, Valerie Robitaille, Vanessa Di Mauro, Venessa Paech, Victoria Burt, Viki Cumberbatch, Will Laco, Zoe O'Brien and countless other community professionals, colleagues and customers I have interacted with throughout the writing process. I wish I could list them all, and I apologize to anyone I have missed. You know who you are—not being named above does not diminish the influence you've had on me.

Once the book took its initial form, I want to thank two special people. Nichole Devolites for her helpful comments and edits, which ensured I didn't miss anything—Nicole, you were a constant confidant and cheerleader, encouraging me every step. I also must endlessly thanks to Carrie Melissa Jones, who not only read the final draft but also provided constructive comments and many meaningful words of encouragement near the end when I needed it most. May you be as lucky to have a friend who is so supportive, caring, and thoughtful. Carrie you've been an inspiration and a north star for me through this process.

After the book was complete, I was happy. But next came the most challenging part: moving from a manuscript to a book. I'd like to thank Gregory Newton Brown. Without his editorial help, this book would never have reached its completed form. I have learned in this process that writing is sometimes the easy part; getting the editing and layout done is often the actual Everest.

Finally, I need to thank my wife, Orit, who, above all else, gave me the support and encouragement to complete this project. Without her endless patience and time, this book would not be the product I am so proud to have put into the world. Community work is hard and having such an understanding partner helps when things don't go as planned or it feels like everyone hates you. My wish for you, reader, is that you find such a great partner to battle the world with as well.

Index

CPSIA information can be obtained
at www.ICGtesting.com
Printed in the USA
BVHW011645220922
647768BV00003B/41